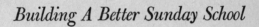

Building A Better Sunday School

Building a Better Sunday School

Through the Weekly Officers and Teachers' Meeting

GAINES S. DOBBINS

Convention Press

NASHVILLE   TENNESSEE

Code Number: Church Study Course

This book is number 1703 in category 17,
section for Adults and Young People.

Library of Congress Catalog Card Number: 57-12145
Printed in the United States of America
5. s 61 R.R.D.

About the Author

GAINES STANLEY DOBBINS, a native Mississippian, received degrees from Mississippi College, the Southern Baptist Theological Seminary, and Columbia University. He served as pastor in Mississippi, then for five years was on the editorial staff of the Baptist Sunday School Board, and for thirty-six years was on the faculty of Southern Seminary, Louisville, Kentucky. In 1956 he joined the faculty of Golden Gate Baptist Theological Seminary, Berkeley, California, with the title of Distinguished Professor of Church Administration.

For four decades Dr. Dobbins has sought to lift the level of teaching and training in Southern Baptist churches. Teaching ministers and other Christian workers in a theological seminary, he has influenced generation after generation of Baptist leaders to give teaching and training a major place in their ministry. In local churches and in assemblies he has touched thousands of lay workers and imparted to them his enthusiasm for qualitative results. He has probably written more Sunday school lesson expositions, more Training Union programs, and more articles dealing with popular religious education than any other living Southern Baptist. His score of books have had national and international circulation.

Dr. Dobbins has served on numerous committees of the Southern Baptist Convention, and is cochairman of the Commission on Bible Study and Membership Training of the Baptist World Alliance. Retiring from the deanship of the School of Religious Education of Southern Seminary, Louisville, Kentucky, Dr. Dobbins, with his wife, now lives at 1451 Thousand Oaks Boulevard, Albany, California.

Contents

Church Study Course

THE CHURCH STUDY COURSE began October 1, 1959. It is a merger of three courses previously promoted by the Sunday School Board—the Sunday School Training Course, the Graded Training Union Study Course, and the Church Music Training Course. On October 1, 1961, the Woman's Missionary Union principles and methods studies were added.

The course is fully graded. The system of awards provides a series of five diplomas of twenty books each for Adults or Young People, two diplomas of five books each for Intermediates, and two diplomas of five books each for Juniors. Book awards earned previously in the Sunday School Training Course, the Graded Training Union Study Course, and the Church Music Training Course may be transferred to the new course.

The course is comprehensive, with books grouped into twenty categories. The purpose of the course is to help Christians to grow in knowledge and conviction, to help them to grow toward maturity in Christian character and competence for service, to encourage them to participate worthily as workers in their churches, and to develop leaders for all phases of church life and work.

The Church Study Course is promoted by the Baptist Sunday School Board, 127 Ninth Avenue, North, Nashville, Tennessee, through its Sunday School, Training Union, Church Music, and Church Administration departments; and the Woman's Missionary Union, 600 North Twentieth Street, Birmingham, Alabama; and by the respective departments in the states affiliated with the Southern Baptist Convention. A complete description of the course and the system of awards may be found in the catalog, *Church Study Course*, which may be obtained without charge from any one of these departments.

A record of all awards earned should be maintained in each church. A person should be designated by the church to keep the files. Forms for such records may be ordered from any Baptist Book Store.

Requirements for Credit in Class or Home Study

IF CREDIT is desired for the study of this book in a class or by home study, the following requirements must be met:

I. IN CLASSWORK

1. The class must meet a minimum of seven and one-half clock hours. The required time does not include assembly periods. Ten class periods of forty-five minutes each are recommended. (If laboratory or clinical work is desired in specialized or technical courses, this requirement may be met by six clock hours of classwork and three clock hours of supervised laboratory or clinical work.)

2. A class member who attends all class sessions and completes the reading of the book within a week following the last class session will not be required to do any written work for credit.

3. A class member who is absent from one or more sessions must answer the questions (pp. 139-140) on all chapters he misses. In such a case, he must turn in his paper within a week, and he must certify that he has read the book.

4. The teacher should request an award for himself. A person who teaches a book in the section for Intermediates or Juniors (any category) or conducts an approved unit of instruction for Nursery, Beginner, or Primary children will be granted an award in category 11, Special Studies, which will count as an elective on his own diploma. He should specify in his request the name of the book taught, or the unit conducted for Nursery, Beginner, or Primary children.

5. The teacher should complete the "Request for Book Awards—Class Study" (Form 150) and forward it within two weeks after the completion of the class to the Church Study Course Awards Office, 127 Ninth Avenue, North, Nashville 3, Tennessee.

II. IN HOME STUDY

1. A person who does not attend any class session may receive credit by answering all questions for written work as indicated in the book (pp. 139-140). When a person turns in his paper on home study, he must certify that he has read the book.

2. Students may find profit in studying the text together, but individual papers are required. Carbon copies or duplicates in any form cannot be accepted.

3. Home study work papers may be graded by the pastor or a person designated by him, or they may be sent to the Church Study Course Awards Office for grading. The form entitled "Request for Book Awards—Home Study" (Form 151) must be used in requesting awards. It should be mailed to Church Study Course Awards Office, 127 Ninth Avenue, North, Nashville 3, Tennessee.

III. CREDIT FOR THIS BOOK

This book is number 1703 in category 17 section for Adults and Young People.

CHAPTER 1

I. A BETTER CHURCH REQUIRES BETTER PERSONS
   1. We Have the Ideal
   2. Let Us Confront the Challenge

II. A SUNDAY SCHOOL IS THE CHURCH AT WORK TEACHING
   1. Neglect of Teaching Corrupted Christianity
   2. Recovery of Teaching Brought Blessings to Baptists

III. A TEACHING CHURCH FOLLOWS THE NEW TESTAMENT PATTERN
   1. The New Testament Provides the Pattern
   2. Baptists Follow the Pattern

IV. THE SUNDAY SCHOOL UNIFIES THE CHURCH PROGRAM
   1. Fragmentation Is a Foe of Unity
   2. Teaching and Learning Furnish a Unifying Ideal

V. THE SUNDAY SCHOOL IMPLEMENTS THE IDEAL
   1. It Affords a Means of Discovery
   2. It Provides a Means of Fulfilment

VI. THE SUNDAY SCHOOL ENLISTS THE CHURCH MEMBERSHIP
   1. It Supplies Service for Every Member
   2. It Enlists Every Member in Service

VII. THE SUNDAY SCHOOL VITALIZES THE CHURCH ACTIVITIES
   1. A Church May Apparently Be Dead
   2. A "Dead" Church May "Come Alive"

VIII. THE SUNDAY SCHOOL PROVIDES A MEANS OF CHURCH CO-OPERATION
   1. Voluntary Co-operation Is a Prized Ideal
   2. Effective Co-operation Can Be a Realized Ideal

IX. THE CHAPTER SUMMARIZED

1

Building Better Sunday Schools
Builds Better Churches

JESUS SAID, "I will build my church." His part as founder and head of the church cannot be improved. He has provided the unchanging pattern, ideals, principles, and purposes according to which his churches are to be built until he comes again. He took his believing, confessing followers into partnership with him in the building of his church. Their part, and ours as their successors, can be indefinitely improved, since we are imperfect and fallible. How to do our part better calls for unceasing search for improvement.

I. A BETTER CHURCH REQUIRES BETTER PERSONS

Certainly churches exist to reach, win, and develop people. No program can be truly Christ-centered and lose sight of the Master's objectives for individual lives.

1. We Have the Ideal

Only saved persons have a right to be church members. Saving souls is the end of all that a church does—but it is the front end! Beyond salvation lie growth and maturity toward the ideal, "Till we all come in the unity of the faith, and of the knowledge of the Son of God, unto a perfect man, unto the measure of the stature of the fulness of Christ" (Eph. 4:13). Like the horizon, this ideal recedes as we approach it.

"Be ye therefore perfect," Jesus challenges us, "even as your Father which is in heaven is perfect" (Matt. 5:48). Paul, one of the most Christlike men of whom we have record, freely confessed that he had not attained unto this ideal of completeness, but said, "I press toward the mark for the prize of the high calling of God in Christ Jesus" (Phil. 3:14). The church is made up of saved sinners who are in the process of becoming better persons.

2. *Let Us Confront the Challenge*

How may a church become a better church? Near the beginning of his ministry, Jesus took his little band of believers into a mountain, sat down with them, and taught them (Matt. 5:1-2). In the great lesson-sermon which followed, he described the kind of persons his followers should be. He explained what they must believe and how they must behave in order to be such persons. He then closed with a vivid picture of possible success or failure in terms of the house that stood and the house that fell, representative of the person who heard and obeyed and the person who heard and did nothing about it.

A strong church consists of taught members who practice what they have learned. Measured by this standard, ought not every church to be a better church? Assuredly there is plenty of room for improvement!

II. A Sunday School Is the Church at Work Teaching

The corollary to the ideal of changed persons must be the emphasis on teaching, since teaching is the process of bringing about desired changes.

1. *Neglect of Teaching Corrupted Christianity*

For some ten centuries—from the fifth to the fifteenth—the teaching ministry of "the church" was neglected and abandoned. This period we call the Dark Ages of Europe and of Christianity. With the Rebirth of Learning (the Renaissance) came the rediscovery of the Bible, its translation from Latin into the language of the people, and the breaking of the grip of Catholicism on the minds and lives of the people.

2. *Recovery of Teaching Brought Blessings to Baptists*

In the forefront of those bringing about this recovery were

Baptists, who contended that "the Holy Scripture is the only sufficient, certain, and infallible rule of all saving knowledge, faith and obedience." * They saw clearly, along with some others, that the Bible must be preached and taught to everyone until the plowman would know the Word of God as well as the priest.

The Sunday school, which had its beginning in England in the latter part of the eighteenth century, was uniquely suited to the needs and purposes of Baptists. It stood for the teaching of the Bible by lay people to lay people. It was not a church-state affair. It was not sponsored or controlled by ecclesiastics. It was thoroughly democratic and concerned for individuals without regard to privilege or position. Baptists of America quickly saw in the Sunday school their best agency for constituting and growing churches.

Southern Baptists particularly adopted the Sunday school as their chief agency, not only in teaching the Bible but in performing almost all the major functions of a church. No human factor more than the Sunday school accounts for the growth, effectiveness, and solidarity of Southern Baptists. In almost all of their churches the Sunday school has been accepted as the church at work carrying out its commission to "go . . . and teach" (Matt. 28:19).

III. A TEACHING CHURCH FOLLOWS THE NEW TESTAMENT PATTERN

How important is the teaching aspect in the ministry of a church? From the New Testament and from history we find the same clear answer.

1. *The New Testament Provides the Pattern*

Matthew pauses twice in his record of Christ's redemptive ministry to tell how he carried it on. Near the beginning, soon after the calling of Peter and Andrew, James and John to be "fishers of men," Jesus "went about all Galilee, teaching

---

* W. J. McGlothlin, "Assembly of Second London Confession of Faith, 1677," *Baptist Confessions of Faith,* American Baptist Publication Society, Philadelphia, 1911.

in their synagogues, and preaching the gospel of the kingdom, and healing all manner of sickness and all manner of disease among the people" (Matt. 4:23). Later Matthew repeats these words verbatim, emphasizing the method of Jesus in the effective communication of his message (Matt. 9:35).

With compassionate concern for the unreached multitudes, Jesus urged those about him to pray for more laborers. He then sent forth the twelve to follow his example, healing, preaching, teaching. He was called "Teacher" more than by any other title. He frequently referred to himself as Teacher. His followers he called "disciples" or learners. His church was essentially a school.

Paul interpreted the mind of Christ in his concept of the church as a school in which the members are learning the lessons of love, of usefulness, of intelligent worship and witness, of effective prayer, of forbearance and gentleness, of humility and decorum (1 Cor. 14).

The churches of the New Testament time and of the first Christian centuries were essentially teaching churches. The "homily" or sermon by a preacher as the center of the service of worship was a later development. No sharp distinction was made between preaching and teaching, between the "laity" and the "clergy." So long as the churches taught, they were powerful and victorious; when they ceased to teach, they became weak and were defeated. Out of their weakness and defeat arose the perversion known to history as the Roman Catholic Church.

2. *Baptists Follow the Pattern*

At no point of polity and practice have our Baptist churches followed the New Testament pattern more closely than in putting teaching and preaching at the center. In this concept the preacher is the principal teacher in the church. As preacher, he instructs and exhorts from the pulpit. As pastor, he is the "overseer" of the teaching ministries of the church, giving encouragement and guidance to those whom the church selects as responsible for its teaching ministries through the Sunday school.

Thus preaching and teaching are not viewed as separate functions but as the two inseparably related means given by Christ himself for achieving the objectives of the church. This program also includes the complementary training function performed by the parallel church agency, the Training Union. Baptists know no other way to build better churches than through this vital combination of preaching-teaching-training. It is the New Testament way of utilizing modern means.

IV. The Sunday School Unifies the Church Program

A church may be the victim of fragmentation. A fragment of its energy may be given to the worship services, another fragment to the several organizations, another fragment to the raising of money, another fragment to evangelism and missions, another fragment to Christian service.

1. Fragmentation Is a Foe of Unity

If the life and work of the church is in a state of fragmentation, pastor and people are liable to become frustrated, dissatisfied, discouraged, unfruitful.

Jesus warned against such futility and anxiety. Paul pled for unity of mind and purpose: "Fulfil ye my joy, that ye be likeminded, having the same love, being of one accord, of one mind" (Phil. 2:1–2). His summons to the Ephesian church was that its members walk worthily of their Christian calling, "endeavouring to keep the unity of the Spirit in the bond of peace;" for "there is one body, and one Spirit, even as ye are called in one hope of your calling; one Lord, one faith, one baptism, one God and Father of all, who is above all, and through all, and in you all" (Eph. 4:3–6). Such unity, however, is not at the expense of individuality, for "unto every one of us is given grace according to the measure of the gift of Christ" (v. 7).

2. Teaching and Learning Furnish a Unifying Ideal

How is this unity in diversity to be maintained in a typical Baptist church? Again we come back to the church as a school. Members and activities may be bound together around the central business of teaching and learning. Concerning everything that is said or done, the question may be asked and answered: What is being taught and learned and what difference does it make?

This unifying ideal becomes the organizing center of the worship services, the teaching and training services, the prayer and praise services, the evangelistic and missionary activities, the money-raising and Christian service enterprises, the fellowship and social occasions, the efforts to reach more people and to provide for adequate building and equipment. Order is thus brought out of confusion; the many parts become related as a whole.

At the heart of such an integrated church program is a well-ordered Sunday school.

V. The Sunday School Implements the Ideal

1. *It Affords a Means of Discovery*

There were as many stars in the heavens before the telescope was invented as there are now, but men could not see them. With every increase in the power of the telescope, astronomers have been able to discover more and more bodies in the sidereal universe. Instruments of discovery are still being perfected with which to expand our celestial outlook.

The Sunday school is the best instrumentality ever devised for discovering unreached multitudes. Like watchers in the sky without a telescope, churches without an effective Sunday school have a narrow range of vision. They can count those on the membership rolls, together with members of their families, but they lack an adequate instrument by means of which to discover the many beyond their immediate notice. They know that Jesus said, "Lift up your eyes, and look on the fields" (John 4:35), but how can they look when the fields stretch afar, unless they have the means of extending their outlook?

2. *It Provides a Means of Fulfilment*

The Sunday school provides the church with the best known means of expanding its outlook and extending its reach. It is axiomatic that pupils must be enrolled before they can be taught. To be enrolled, they must be discovered—chiefly through the religious census. Discovery opens the way to friendly visits; these visits develop friendships; friends like to get together, and the Sunday school department and class furnish an attractive basis of association and a strong bond of attachment.

Persons who have found the joy of fellowship in Bible study and service share their satisfactions with others, and they in turn with others, and they with still others. In ever-enlarging circles this process of sharing approaches more and more the standard of Jesus, who said, "Ye shall be witnesses unto me both in Jerusalem, and in all Judaea, and in Samaria, and unto the uttermost part of the earth" (Acts 1:8).

VI. THE SUNDAY SCHOOL ENLISTS THE CHURCH MEMBERSHIP

How can the church enlist every member in the world enterprise to reach for Christ every possible person everywhere? Through the Sunday school, as the church at work teaching, this end can be achieved more certainly and more fruitfully than through any other agency known to Christian history or to contemporary Christianity.

1. *It Supplies Service for Every Member*

Christians are saved to serve. Jesus said, "My Father worketh hitherto, and I work" (John 5:17). We are not saved by good works but we are saved for good works. "For by grace are ye saved through faith; and that not of yourselves: it is the gift of God: not of works, lest any man should boast" (Eph. 2:8–9). But in the next breath Paul declares: "For we are his workmanship, created in Christ Jesus unto good works, which God hath before ordained that we should walk in them" (v. 10).

The soul of the idle Christian will be saved if he has indeed trusted Christ, but his usefulness and reward can be lost. The most baffling problem which most of our churches confront is that of the multitude of unenlisted church members. Perhaps many of these idle Christians are not altogether blameworthy. They may have begun well but became cold and indifferent because of neglect. Their cry may be that of the laborers who stood idle in the market place, "No man hath hired us" (Matt. 20:7).

2. It Enlists Every Member in Service

A church with a well-organized and properly graded Sunday school leaves without excuse those who are unenlisted. Somewhere there is a place of useful service for every member. Everyone can be enlisted in Bible study, whether or not it is possible for him to attend on Sunday. Everyone who attends can participate in the lesson discussion.

Everyone, except perhaps some shut-ins, can help discover the people to be reached and can take part in visiting them. Everyone can support the church enterprise, including the Sunday school, through tithes and offerings. Everyone can pray and bear witness. There are many forms of specialized service according to interest and aptitude—officers, teachers, musicians, class officers, or visitors.

The Sunday school not only affords a great variety of places of service, it also offers training and fellowship in service. No Christian need feel lonely or isolated in his ministry. The work of the Sunday school is a partnership. It brings together officers, teachers, and other workers as a team in the most important and fascinating endeavor in the world—that of defeating Satan and winning for Christ. The warfare will not be easy, but with Christ we are bound to win: "In the world ye shall have tribulation; but be of good cheer; I have overcome the world" (John 16:33).

Paul thus magnifies and encourages our enlistment in Christian service: "For we are labourers together with God: ye are God's husbandry, ye are God's building" (1 Cor. 3:9). The Sunday school makes it possible for every Christian to realize these high ideals through enlistment in service for Christ's sake through the church.

VII. The Sunday School Vitalizes the Church Activities

"Mother, what is *dead*?" asked little four-year-old Marjorie when her puppy had been run over and killed by a passing automobile. Patiently her mother tried to explain that "dead" means the absence of life. "Then are the trees dead when the leaves and fruit are gone?" Marjorie persisted. Again Mother explained that what seems lifeless is really alive on the inside but must have the warm sunshine and rain to bring leaves and fruit again.

1. *A Church May Apparently Be Dead*

When applied to a church, "What is dead?" A particular church may lose an increasing percentage of its members, until one day it ceases to exist. Its closed doors and broken windows may bear mute evidence to the absence of life. Much more often, however, a church that seems dead is more like the tree in the wintertime—within is life that needs only right conditions in order to reappear and bear fruit. Often a church in a dormant state will "come alive" if proper conditions are provided.

2. *A "Dead" Church May "Come Alive"*

A well-organized and functioning Sunday school can make the difference between a dead or dying church and a living, fruit-bearing church. Paul compares the church to the human body. The health, indeed the life, of the body depends on the healthful functioning of its many members working together harmoniously. A good Sunday school provides the conditions both of nourishment and of exercise for every member of the church body. The several departments with their classes are like living cells that furnish life and growth for the whole.

The Sunday school is not the whole church, to be sure, but it provides conditions according to which the whole church is vitalized. When the Sunday school officers and teachers come together week by week to plan and to study, to worship and to work, the life stream of the church is enriched and its health is practically guaranteed. Like a healthy body that can throw off infection when attacked, a healthy, teaching church can resist the enemies to its life, whether they attack from without or from within.

VIII. THE SUNDAY SCHOOL PROVIDES A MEANS OF CHURCH CO-OPERATION

Co-operation is a most meaningful Baptist word. It is always associated with another significant word, *voluntary*.

1. *Voluntary Co-operation Is a Prized Ideal*

Throughout their history, Baptists have resisted any form of overlordship of the churches or coercion of their members. Independence and interdependence, rightly related, account for our marvelous spirit of unity. We recognize no authority in religion except that of Christ and the Scriptures. Yet we are held together in strong bonds of unity because of common faith and experience, common polity and practice, common worship and work, common study and service.

2. *Effective Co-operation Can Be a Realized Ideal*

How is this doctrine of voluntary co-operation to be given practical expression? Again, in the Sunday school we find an effective answer. Here one group works together in the interest of little children; another seeks to serve the older children; another concentrates attention on Intermediates; another devotes its energies to the leadership of Young People; still another gives attention to the welfare of Adults; and in all of these groups there are those who are responsible for administration and related ministries. Yet these various groups, constituting the leadership of the Sunday school, form a team with the spirit of "all for each and each for all."

With this team spirit dominant among the Sunday school officers and teachers, the spirit of the church as a whole is bound to be co-operative. There will, of course, be honest differences of opinion, but they will be resolved prayerfully and intelligently. "We are not divided, all one body we," may be sung with the spirit and with the understanding.

Such co-operation, one of the most important elements in the success of a church, must not be left to chance. Churches that have tried it bear witness that the coming together of officers and teachers each week for fellowship in planning and preparation is the most successful way known to develop and maintain effective co-operation. They declare that whatever a church may do, it will probably do it better if there is a weekly officers and teachers' meeting. The size of the church does not determine the outcome. A few officers and teachers in a small Sunday school can develop needed teamwork just as surely as the larger number in the big church.

IX. The Chapter Summarized

1. A better church requires better persons. A strong church consists of taught members who practice what they have learned.

2. A Sunday school is the church at work teaching. Uniquely suited to the needs and purposes of Baptists, the school of the church stands for the teaching of the Bible by lay people to lay people.

3. A teaching church follows the New Testament pattern. Baptists build better churches through the vital combination of preaching-teaching-training.

4. The Sunday school unifies the church program. Members and activities are bound together around the center of teaching and learning.

5. The Sunday school enlists the church membership. The ideal of every-member enlistment may be realized through the teaching church.

6. The Sunday school vitalizes the church activities. Officers and teachers meeting week by week for planning and study provide conditions necessary to the church's health.

7. The Sunday school provides a means of church co-operation. The weekly officers and teachers' meeting furnishes the plan for effectiveness in working together.

CHAPTER 2

I. THE WEEKLY OFFICERS AND TEACHERS' MEETING SUPPLIES THE NEED OF THE CLASS SUNDAY SCHOOL

1. Advantages Outweigh Difficulties
2. Obstacles Can Be Overcome

II. THE WEEKLY OFFICERS AND TEACHERS' MEETING SUPPLIES THE NEED OF THE DEPARTMENT SUNDAY SCHOOL

1. Teamwork Is Essential
2. Desired Values Are Attainable

III. THE WEEKLY OFFICERS AND TEACHERS' MEETING SUPPLIES THE NEED OF FELLOWSHIP

1. Fellowship Is a Vital Factor
2. Fellowship Is Maintained Through Association

IV. THE WEEKLY OFFICERS AND TEACHERS' MEETING SUPPLIES THE NEED OF PLANNING

1. Planning Is a Co-operative Process
2. Co-operative Planning Is Achieved Through the Weekly Officers and Teachers' Meeting

V. THE WEEKLY OFFICERS AND TEACHERS' MEETING SUPPLIES THE NEED OF SHARING

1. Friendship Is Essential to Sharing
2. Friendliness Is Developed Through the Workers' Meeting

VI. OBJECTIONS TO THE WEEKLY OFFICERS AND TEACHERS' MEETING CAN BE OVERCOME

1. External Difficulties Can Be Met
2. Internal Problems Can Be Solved

VII. THE CHAPTER SUMMARIZED

2

Every Sunday School Can Have a
Weekly Officers and Teachers' Meeting

EVERY CHURCH can be a better church. Since improvement can be obtained and maintained chiefly through the Sunday school, every church should seek to have a better Sunday school. Achievement of this objective involves the meeting of certain basic needs. Whatever the size or location or peculiar condition of the Sunday school, its needs remain much the same. Let us look at a tried and proved way of supplying these needs.

I. THE WEEKLY OFFICERS AND TEACHERS' MEETING SUPPLIES THE NEED OF THE CLASS SUNDAY SCHOOL

The majority of Southern Baptist churches have fewer than three hundred members. Many of these churches worship and study in one-room buildings or in buildings with a few added rooms. Their Sunday schools are organized by classes rather than by departments. Too often it has been assumed that these class Sunday schools do not need and cannot maintain a weekly officers and teachers' meeting.

1. Advantages Outweigh Difficulties

"Ours is a small Sunday school with one or two classes for each of the age groups. Can we have a successful officers and teachers' meeting?" The answer is an emphatic yes! Pastor, superintendent, associate superintendent, general secretary, musicians, and ten to fifteen teachers add up to about a score of persons responsible for the teaching program of their church. Sometimes the number may be fewer, in many cases it will be greater. In almost any case there will be more

13

than are required for a baseball nine or a football eleven! As well say that these players do not need to get together for practice as to say that the officers and teachers of a small Sunday school do not need to get together for planning and preparation!

Let us view the matter negatively. Suppose the workers in a class school do not come together in a weekly meeting; what happens? On Sunday morning they are not acquainted with the pastor's plans, nor is he acquainted with the plans of the officers and teachers. Obviously they cannot work together for maximum effectiveness in making the teaching service and the preaching service support each other.

The general superintendent has no opportunity to confer with his fellow workers as to plans for the assembly programs, the carrying out of any special plans, or the reaching of absentees and prospective members. The superintendent may drift into the role of a "master of ceremonies" for a few minutes on Sunday morning, repeating a form that becomes monotonous and unattractive.

The secretary may post the number present and the amount of the collection; even the percentages on the record system may be indicated. Yet this procedure Sunday after Sunday makes the secretary more of a calculating machine than a purposeful recorder and reporter of what is taking place.

The musicians, instead of planning carefully to make the music an essential feature of the teaching-learning situation, may come simply prepared to use whatever hymns are haphazardly selected.

Teachers will be in the worst plight of all—no one will know what the other is planning to do. There is no way to concentrate on common objectives. Problems of common concern cannot be dealt with. There is no stimulus of mind meeting mind in the study of the Bible. All too often, personal preparation is inadequate; purposes and results of teaching are not compared; and what is "learned" has very little chance of being given expression.

2. Obstacles Can Be Overcome

Consider how every one of the weaknesses named in the foregoing can be given attention when officers and teachers come together each week for prayer, planning, and preparation. It is clearly a mistaken idea that such a meeting is not practicable because the Sunday school is relatively small and has classes rather than departments. In many, if not most cases, the weekly officers and teachers' meeting would bring about growth that soon would call for departments and thus raise the organizational level. As a matter of fact, some of the best officers and teachers' meetings being held are by smaller Sunday schools, with results that fully demonstrate both the possibility and the value of the meeting.

The superintendent of a Sunday school in a rural church with a part-time pastor became convinced of the need and the value of the weekly officers and teachers' meeting. The teachers lived at distances from the church and objected that they could not come because of lack of transportation. The superintendent made the rounds in his car, gathered the officers and teachers, and transported them to the church week after week until the meeting became firmly established.

A pastor of two rural churches, who had a conviction of the need and value of the weekly officers and teachers' meeting, furnished the necessary leadership by arranging for the officers and teachers to meet an hour before prayer meeting on Wednesday in one church, on Tuesday in the other. A seminary student pastor, who could be on the field only Saturday and Sunday, planned the meeting of officers and teachers for late Saturday afternoon.

Once the practicability and value of the meeting have been established, the burden of leadership may be shared with the officers and teachers themselves, thus relieving the pastor and superintendent of undue responsibility. Given a pastor and a superintendent with conviction and determination, a successful weekly officers and teachers' meeting is possible anywhere.

II. THE WEEKLY OFFICERS AND TEACHERS' MEETING SUPPLIES THE NEED OF THE DEPARTMENT SUNDAY SCHOOL

The larger the school, the more imperative becomes the necessity for "togetherness." It is assumed that when a Sunday school grows large enough and has the required space, it will be departmentized.

1. *Teamwork Is Essential*

The advantages of the department school are too obvious to be argued; yet there is inevitably some loss of the sense of "togetherness" found in the class school where all ages meet in one assembly.

The several age groups in a department school are necessarily isolated from one another. The workers with the little children may have almost no contact with those who work with the older children. The children's workers may know nothing of what goes on in the Intermediate department. Workers with children and Intermediates may lose all touch with those who serve in the Young People's and Adult departments. Adult workers may lose sight of all others except themselves. The gain of "separateness" may involve the loss of "togetherness."

"How can we have a worth-while officers and teachers' meeting when we work with different age groups, use different literature, teach different lessons, and have different objectives?" The very statement of difficulties in terms of "differences" emphasizes the importance of the weekly meeting.

Again, suppose there is no such meeting. The very size of the corps of officers and teachers makes it increasingly impossible for the pastor to give them his leadership. With a superintendent for each department, the general superintendent often feels that he is without a job. The general secretary works with a staff of department secretaries, but the results of their figuring are often all but thrown away because there is no occasion when the reports can be publicized, studied, and made of value for better attendance and teaching. Individual departments may do excellent work, but the school as a whole, serving the church as a whole, suffers inevitable loss of common purpose and mobilized power.

2. Desired Values Are Attainable

On the other hand, every interest of the Sunday school may be furthered by the coming together each week of the officers and teachers. Perhaps the pastor gains most of all. As the bishop or overseer or "chief of staff," the pastor can fulfil his calling as administrator of the teaching program of the church in a way to match his responsibility as preacher and leader of worship. How better can the minister give guidance to the church's teaching ministry than by identifying himself with the officers and teachers of the Sunday school in their weekly meeting for preparation to teach the Word?

To the minister of education, if the church is so fortunate as to have one, the opportunities of the officers and teachers' meeting are priceless. Without such a meeting he would be like a coach who meets the team only on the playing field, or like a general who directs the army only after the battle begins.

An effective weekly officers and teachers' meeting restores the general superintendent to his place of leadership as a true supervisor. It gives him the opportunity to build the school and improve its operation by strategic planning that can be communicated to those to whom the plans are entrusted. The general secretary can make the records come alive as instruments of improvement, enlargement, enlistment. Department superintendents find their work broadened and deepened, with informed and co-operative teachers and associates through whom the work of the department can be efficiently carried on. Teachers are immeasurably enriched as they find themselves comrades of others who are like-minded, with whom they can share as members of the teaching team.

Those who gain the most are, of course, the class members, as from better prepared officers and teachers they receive "the holy scriptures, which are able to make . . . wise unto salvation through faith which is in Christ Jesus" (2 Tim. 3:15). No Sunday school is so large or so well organized as to justify dispensing with this weekly meeting of officers and teachers.

III. THE WEEKLY OFFICERS AND TEACHERS' MEETING SUPPLIES THE NEED OF FELLOWSHIP

"Resigners" are the near-despair of ministers and Sunday school superintendents. Studies indicate that the average term of service of the typical Sunday school officer or teacher is about three years.

1. *Fellowship Is a Vital Factor*

Of course there are legitimate reasons why workers resign, such as ill health, inescapable Sunday duties, removal from the community. The heartbreaking aspect of this wasteful turnover arises from the "quitters" who give up not so much because of necessity as from discouragement.

The officer or teacher may become disheartened because of decline in interest and attendance, or because of a sense of personal inadequacy, or because of sheer loneliness in carrying heavy responsibility without the sense of fellowship. Teaching and preparing to teach may become an almost unbearably lonely task when the operation is repeated Sunday after Sunday, month after month, without the encouragement of companionship.

Good executives know that group work greatly increases the satisfaction of the worker and his output. In industry arrangements are made, often at great expense to the company, for the workers to eat together, to play together, to discuss their problems together. Business concerns arrange for regular and frequent staff meetings, at company expense. Valuable time is spent in exchange of ideas, instruction in better methods, and inspiration to increased production in shorter time with less expense and greater profit. Every teacher in a public school or in an institution of higher learning knows the absolute necessity of well-planned and well-conducted faculty meetings. Solitary workers in any calling or profession today are few and generally inefficient.

2. Fellowship Is Maintained Through Association

If there were no other reason for the officers and teachers' meeting, its supply of the need for fellowship would justify it. We read of the Jerusalem Christians that they "did eat their meat with gladness and singleness of heart," breaking bread with one another "from house to house." These first Christians had no houses of worship; for the most part they met in one another's homes. The common meal bound them together in closer ties of Christian fellowship.

The church house today may well perform the same function, as the officers and teachers of the Sunday school are brought together to "eat their meat with gladness and singleness of heart." With such a program it has usually followed, as a matter of course, that "the Lord added to the church daily such as should be saved" (Acts 2:47). There is a clear relation between fellowship and evangelism, the coming together of the workers and the blessing of God upon their work.

IV. The Weekly Officers and Teachers' Meeting Supplies the Need of Planning

A noted educational philosopher has said, "Acting with an aim is all one with acting intelligently." Purposefulness is indeed a test of intelligence—the ability to look ahead, foresee difficulties as well as opportunities, and make long-range plans for desired results. Do not many of our gravest failures come from lack of adequate planning?

1. Planning Is a Co-operative Process

The pastor may sit in his study and make some excellent plans for the Sunday school; but how can he communicate them? He may present certain of his ideas and ideals occasionally from the pulpit; but he will be wise not to take the worship period too often for promotional purposes.

The minister of education, or the general superintendent,

or the department superintendents, or the general secretary may have valuable plans or troublesome problems to present. If there is no meeting for planning together, these leaders may go to individuals one at a time, or they may write letters, or they may put statements in the church bulletin, but they will often feel like one who calls number after number on the telephone only to get the "busy signal." By the time the word eventually gets around, the occasion may have passed, or interest may have grown cold.

2. *Co-operative Planning Is Achieved Through the Weekly Officers and Teachers' Meeting*

The weekly officers and teachers' meeting affords an un-paralleled opportunity for the proposal of plans, the discussion and refinement of these plans and the putting of the plans into action.

It is axiomatic that people do not generally take to plans which they have had no part in helping to make. Often keen disappointment has come to the pastor, or the minister of education, or the general superintendent, when plans that were developed with great care have been ignored and even opposed by those to whom they were announced. The mistake was not in the wisdom of the plan but in the failure to develop it co-operatively. When the officers and teachers can say, "our plan," not "his plan" or "their plan," achievement is assured. How else can such planning be effectively done if there is no weekly meeting of the most responsible group in the church, the Sunday school officers and teachers?

The Sunday school which maintains a weekly officers and teachers' meeting affords the church its best instrumentality for united planning.

V. The Weekly Officers and Teachers' Meeting Supplies the Need of Sharing

Teaching has been defined as "friendship with a purpose." Learning takes place best in an atmosphere of friendliness.

Preaching is most effective when the minister and the congregation are friends.

1. *Friendship Is Essential to Sharing*

Dr. John A. Broadus, great preacher and teacher of preachers, was once asked, "What are the essentials of a good sermon?" He replied: "There are three: first, a friendly, responsive congregation; second, a friendly, responsive congregation; third, a friendly, responsive congregation." Is not this likewise an essential of a good lesson—a friendly, responsive class? A teacher concerned only to "teach the lesson" will almost always have an indifferent class. Lack of warmth and friendliness in the relation of teacher to class blocks learning more effectually than lack of teaching skill.

Friendliness cannot be feigned. It must be genuine or it will tarnish and its counterfeit nature will be known. How can the leaders of the Sunday school develop and maintain this genuineness of friendliness without which all their efforts are discounted?

"A man that hath friends must shew himself friendly" (Prov. 18:24). How may he "show himself friendly?" By sharing! The family that shares its vegetables and flowers with neighbors is known to be friendly. The church that freely shares its spiritual values with others is proved to be friendly. The minister or teacher who shares himself with congregation or class is exhibiting "friendship with a purpose." Yet such friendliness will not shine forth on Sunday if it has been hidden under a bushel during the week!

2. *Friendliness Is Developed Through the Workers' Meeting*

The superintendent, pastor, and minister of education, along with the others who gather about them as officers and teachers, cultivate and refresh the spirit of friendliness when they come together between Sundays for the purpose of sharing. In the officers and teachers' meeting they share themselves, their experiences, their ideas, their problems, their disappointments, their aspirations, their successes, their plans and purposes. In this process of sharing they develop strong bonds of friendship for one another. The difficulties of one become the difficulties of all; the achievements of one become the achievements of all.

From such an atmosphere of friendliness, officers and teachers will go before their departments and classes with contagious friendliness. This spirit immediately becomes a chief contributing factor to fruitful teaching and learning. From such an experience of friendly sharing in the departments and classes, the people will go into the service of worship and form a "friendly, responsive congregation" to whom the minister can preach with confidence and effectiveness. Meeting together week by week, members of the staff of officers and teachers realize that each is significant and necessary. Frederick W. Farrar has said,

> I am only one,
> But I am one.
> I can not do everything,
> But I can do something.
> What I can do
> I ought to do;
> And what I ought to do
> By the grace of God I will do.

VI. Objections to the Weekly Officers and Teachers' Meeting Can Be Overcome

Because its leaders have assumed that the obstacles in the way of the weekly officers and teachers' meeting are too great to be surmounted, many a Sunday school is limping along when it might be striding forward. That there are difficulties cannot be denied, but that they are insuperable should be challenged. What are some of the objections raised, and how are they to be met?

1. External Difficulties Can Be Met

"Our officers and teachers do not have time to attend." It is readily admitted that time is precious and many demands are made on our time. Yet, when the officer or teacher was elected to this highly responsible post in the church, was it not understood that the task would take time? Assuming that the barest minimum would be two hours of preparation for the hour of Sunday service, how better could one of those hours be spent than in co-operative study? Officers and teachers testify that the midweek hour spent together actually saves time. Planned work can always be done more quickly and easily than unplanned work. Planning with others is not time lost, it is time saved.

"Many of our officers and teachers work late, and so cannot get to the meeting on time." The schedule of the meeting must, of course, be adjusted to the time of the people. If Wednesday is the day when places of business are closed in the afternoon, thus creating an attendance problem, why not shift both officers and teachers' meeting and prayer meeting to Thursday?

If there is not time to go home for the evening meal and then get to the church in time for the meeting, why not have a "family meal" at the church? If the time of the officers and teachers' meeting comes too close to that of the prayer meeting, why not adjust the schedule so as to share the time available? It remains true that where there's a will there's a way!

"We do not have the leadership necessary to the success of the meeting." This objection involves a misconception as to the nature of the weekly officers and teachers' meeting. Its purpose is not to bring together listeners to a lecture or auditors to the teaching of next Sunday's lesson. Any group of officers and teachers are, by their very selection, qualified to pray together, plan together, discuss their problems and needs together, and share in the preparation of the lesson or lessons to be taught.

Any superintendent can profitably spend time preparing the program and plan sheets for guiding the group study. The very fact that outstanding leadership is not available for the conduct of the meeting is in reality an advantage, since responsibility then falls on the rank and file of the officer-teacher group, who will develop in leadership as they exercise their gifts in the process of sharing.

Perhaps there is, at this point, need for rethinking our concepts of the qualifications of department superintendents and of the general superintendent of the class Sunday school. The superintendent is elected, not only to administrative duties, but also to the responsibility of developing teachers.

True, he must know Sunday school organization and administration. But he must know the fundamentals of good teaching. He should be able to appraise the teaching being done in the classes and analyze its strong points and its weak points. He should be able to direct the teaching improvement periods in such a way as to encourage the teachers to share their strong points with others, and to guide those with weak points to sources of help.

A superintendent may gain a working knowledge of good teaching through prayerful observation of the procedures in the classes and through noting the participation of the teachers in the discussions in the weekly meeting, provided he relates his observation to a study of the principles of teaching. Every department superintendent should master the teaching books in category 17 of the Church Study Course. These include the teaching book for the age group which he leads, and such general studies as *The Improvement of Teaching in the Sunday School, When Do Teachers Teach, Teaching to Win and Develop, Looking at Learning, Jesus the Teacher, Preparing to Teach the Bible,* and others. Many other good books in the field should be available through the church library.

2. *Internal Problems Can Be Solved*

"We use Graded Lessons, hence the teaching of no one lesson will help us all." This objection indicates another mistaken idea as to the purpose of the meeting. It is not to provide teachers with a ready-made teaching plan for next Sunday; rather, it is to help teachers to better preparation of their own lesson plans. The procedure for department meetings where the closely Graded Lessons are used will be dealt with in a later chapter. Suffice it to say now that some of the best officers and teachers' meetings are those where the closely Graded Lessons are used.

"Some of our best teachers say they do not need the help of the meeting; they prefer to make preparation alone." Do not these seasoned and competent teachers miss the point? The very fact of their ability should give them a sense of obligation to share with the less experienced and less competent teachers who need their help. Theirs should be the compulsion of *noblesse oblige*, "rank imposes obligation." In the words of Jesus: "For unto whomsoever much is given, of him shall be much required: and to whom men have committed much, of him will they ask the more" (Luke 12:48).

The competent teacher who comes to share with those less fortunate will find his own competence increased and his influence multiplied. James Russell Lowell reminds us it is "not what we give, but what we share" that is most pleasing to Christ. The Master Teacher used the twelve to help him teach and shared with them his message and his method.

"The weekly meeting of officers and teachers places too great a burden on the pastor, the minister of education, the general superintendent." The meeting, properly planned and conducted, should lighten rather than increase the burden of responsibility of these administrative officers. Their rule should be that of all good administrators: not to do themselves what they can get others to do. Their best opportunity for division of labor comes through this weekly meeting when they have at hand those through whom they must work anyway, instead of having to seek them out. Ministers and superintendents have generally found that the officers and teachers' meeting saves much time and energy, reduces lost motion and frustration, adds to spiritual power and effectiveness, and guarantees a prayer service that vitalizes the whole church program.

"We don't get enough out of the meeting to justify it." This is the crowning objection, and it must be faced frankly and intelligently. If those who attend are not profited, the meeting is obviously not worth maintaining. The same thing can be said about any other meeting of the church. There are members of classes who have quit coming to Sunday school because they claimed "they did not get enough out of it." There are members of the church who give this as their reason for not attending the services of worship. Shall we therefore disband our classes, and close the church doors? Certainly not!

We continue to do two things: We seek continuously to improve the teaching and preaching services; and we try to convince the objectors that they cannot get without giving. This must be our twofold answer to those who say they do not get much from the officers and teachers' meeting. We must unceasingly strive to improve the meeting; and we must convince the objectors that they must invest in it if they expect to derive profit from it. How to make the meeting worth while is the object of our next studies.

We shall consider the planning, administration, and promotion which must go into initiating and maintaining a weekly meeting, and then center attention on the teaching improvement aspect.

VII. THE CHAPTER SUMMARIZED

1. The weekly officers and teachers' meeting supplies the need of the class Sunday school. The small school needs and can have a successful weekly meeting.

2. The weekly officers and teachers' meeting supplies the need of the department Sunday school. The larger and more complex the organization, the more indispensable becomes the weekly meeting.

3. The weekly officers and teachers' meeting supplies the need for fellowship. Workers in any enterprise serve better when they have the sense of vital partnership.

4. The weekly officers and teachers' meeting supplies the need of planning. Working together calls for planning together and planned work is always better work.

5. The weekly officers and teachers' meeting supplies the need of sharing. Friendship developed through shared interests creates a friendly atmosphere in which teaching and preaching are made more effective.

6. Objections to the weekly officers and teachers' meeting can be overcome. There are difficulties, of course, but they can be met through determination, reasonableness, and kindness.

CHAPTER 3

I. THE CHURCH SHOULD BE LED TO ESTABLISH THE MEETING
   1. Church Control Follows an Established Policy
   2. Church Control Stabilizes the Weekly Officers and Teachers' Meeting

II. OFFICERS AND TEACHERS SHOULD BE CONVINCED OF THE NEED
   1. Unconvinced Workers Invite Failure
   2. Convinced Workers Assure Success

III. THE PURPOSE OF THE MEETING SHOULD BE CLARIFIED
   1. The Meeting Is Necessary
   2. The Meeting Is a Profitable Investment

IV. PERSONS EXPECTED TO ATTEND SHOULD BE IDENTIFIED
   1. Specific Persons Are Involved
   2. Specific Purposes and Procedures Are Proposed

V. TIME AND SCHEDULE SHOULD BE CONSIDERED
   1. The Schedule Is Related to the Prayer Meeting
   2. The Schedule Considers Local Conditions

VI. DIFFICULTIES OF ATTENDANCE SHOULD BE CONFRONTED
   1. Difficulties of Nonattendance Must Be Faced
   2. Difficulties of Irregular Attendance Can Be Met

VII. PRACTICAL PROBLEMS CAN BE SOLVED
   1. Problems of the Fellowship Meal Can Be Solved
   2. Problems of Leadership and Opposition Can Be Solved

VIII. THE CHAPTER SUMMARIZED

3

The Officers and Teachers' Meeting
Requires Purposeful Planning

THE teaching ministry of a church is of tremendous importance. Those who give it guidance cannot afford to risk failure. The complexities and competitions of modern life confront us with many problems. Success in enrolling ever-increasing numbers of persons in our Sunday schools should both rejoice and disturb us. We must match growth with improvement, else growth may cease or overgrowth bring collapse. On the human side, purposeful planning is demanded. As we have seen, the weekly officers and teachers' meeting provides the means for this planning of the church educational program. The meeting for planning must itself be planned, with clear-cut and resolute purpose. Not to plan thus is to invite frustration and failure.

Let us look at certain prerequisites to the success of the weekly officers and teachers' meeting.

I. THE CHURCH SHOULD BE LED TO ESTABLISH THE MEETING

Through all the stages of their development the Sunday school Standards have specified that the church shall elect the officers and teachers and the school shall report regularly to the church.

1. *Church Control Follows an Established Policy*

Few, if any, Baptist Sunday schools would undertake to operate independently of the churches to which they belong. Long ago our Sunday schools gave up electing their own officers and teachers, financing themselves separately, and determining their policies independently.

The same principle holds in respect to the officers and teachers' meeting. A service of such far-reaching importance is not the concern of Sunday school officers and teachers alone; it is properly the responsibility of the whole church. The church should be led to understand and appreciate the plans and purposes of the meeting, the values and difficulties involved, and the relation of the meeting to the total ministries of the church.

2. Church Control Stabilizes the Weekly Officers and Teachers' Meeting

The principle of church control applied to the officers and teachers' meeting will mean: (1) the setting up of such a meeting by authority of the church; (2) the establishment by the church of the policy regarding attendance on the meeting by church-elected officers and teachers of the Sunday school; (3) approval by the church of the plans and purposes of the meeting; (4) church approval of the leadership and schedule of the meeting; (5) the financial support of the meeting when legitimate expenses are incurred; (6) the recognition of the church officers who are responsible for the meeting—pastor, minister of education, general superintendent of the Sunday school, and such others as may be named; (7) the making of regular reports of the meeting to the church by its officers. A long step will be taken toward the initiation and the maintenance of the weekly officers and teachers' meeting when it is thus church sponsored and church controlled.

II. OFFICERS AND TEACHERS SHOULD BE CONVINCED OF THE NEED

The degree of conviction held by the workers regarding the value of the meeting will account for its success or failure.

1. Unconvinced Workers Invite Failure

The pastor of a church with a growing Sunday school became convinced that there should be a weekly meeting of officers and teachers. The general superintendent somewhat hesitantly agreed with him. They called together the superintendents of the departments and several influential teachers, to whom they announced their intention. The pastor spoke warmly in favor of the meeting from the pulpit on Sunday and at prayer meeting. The date was set for the first meeting of the officers and teachers. The pastor was embarrassed and hurt when fewer than a dozen made their appearance. After a few weeks, when even this attendance declined, the matter was dropped, and the pastor sadly admitted defeat.

In another situation, the feasibility and the values of the officers and teachers' meeting were convincingly presented by a state Sunday school worker. Inspired by the speaker's enthusiasm, officers and teachers voted to begin such a meeting. At first there was gratifying attendance; then interest gradually lessened and attendance declined to a vanishing point. Now, when the subject is mentioned there is a shaking of heads and the comment, "We tried it once—it just doesn't work!"

Almost invariably, when establishing or maintaining the meeting has failed, the disappointment stems from lack of conviction on the part of officers and teachers that the meeting supplies a vital need. Will not such a lack account for the failure of almost any enterprise?

2. Convinced Workers Assure Success

It is not enough for a few leaders to see the need—it must be consciously felt by those whose support is necessary for success. The question is not primarily, "Is it a good thing?" but rather, "Will it be worth what it costs?" When officers and teachers are convinced that coming together week by week will build a better Sunday school and church, will benefit departments and classes, and will result in greater satisfactions to teachers and pupils, their realization of value received will guarantee success of the plan.

Concerning any important venture, practical-minded men and women ask, What is it for? Land is cleared for the purpose of producing food; factories are built to accomplish the manufacture of goods; railroads, buses, and airplanes are made in order to provide transportation; schools are set up to furnish education; churches exist to propagate religion. Concerning the weekly officers and teachers' meeting, the question is properly raised, What will it accomplish?

III. The Purpose of the Meeting Should Be Clarified

The question may be frankly raised, Why add another church meeting? Sunday school officers and teachers are almost always engaged in other church activities. Some are deacons; some serve on committees; the women should be in the Woman's Missionary Union and the men in the Baptist Brotherhood. There are those who sing in the choir. All should be in the Training Union. Visitation and personal service and witnessing require time. Associational meetings must be attended.

The cry of overwork goes up from honest hearts of faithful members who may even complain that they are neglecting their homes in the service of the church. Not always are these complaints justified; but to the extent that they have a basis in fact, they should be given careful consideration when an additional weekly meeting is proposed.

1. *The Meeting Is Necessary*

If the coming together of officers and teachers is just another meeting, it can scarcely be defended. Its justification is that of a family which comes together at mealtime for the fellowship and food necessary to carry on all their other duties. Its necessity is that of the driver who stops regularly at the filling station for refueling. Its value is that of the general's conference with his lieutenants before going into battle. Its purpose is that of Jesus when he drew his disciples apart for instruction and inspiration before they went forth to be his witnesses.

The coming together of officers and teachers each week is a center about which may gather many of the functions of the church. While preparation for the teaching of next Sunday's lessons is important, this is but one of the major purposes of the meeting.

2. The Meeting Is a Profitable Investment

The weekly officers and teachers' meeting provides opportunity for correlation of other meetings, thus actually reducing the number that might otherwise be required. It serves to concentrate attention on related responsibilities and actually saves time through careful and intelligent planning. It brings together those who have common duties and implements the principle that "many hands make light work." It enables the Sunday school leaders to spotlight the objectives which call for united effort.

The weekly officers and teachers' meeting serves to emphasize the ideal of the church as a family, with parents and children present for the fellowship meal. Varied activities may be planned for persons other than Sunday school officers and teachers, and for participation in the hour of prayer that follows. This meeting may be to the prayer meeting what the Sunday school is to the morning worship service and what the Training Union is to the evening worship service.

Leading workers to a broadened concept of the purposes of the weekly officers and teachers' meeting will often be a gradual process. Not every church can include all the purposes suggested. Some churches may go beyond those which have been indicated. Local conditions must be taken into account in determining the pattern. The essential matter, at this point, is to realize the centrality of this meeting of officers and teachers, along with the prayer meeting, in the life and work of the church and to define its purposes broadly and specifically. These specific objectives and functions will be dealt with in detail in a succeeding chapter.

IV. Persons Expected to Attend Should Be Identified

When officers and teachers agree to serve in the Sunday school, what commitments should they be expected to make? The seriousness of their responsibility calls for a clear understanding of the obligations assumed. It would ordinarily be a mistake to demand attendance on the weekly officers and teachers' meeting as a condition of election. A better approach is to present such attendance as a contribution to the success of the worker. "We want you to attend because we want you to be happy and successful in your work," may be sincerely said. "If you cannot avail yourself of this help," may be frankly added, "we doubt our right to ask you to take the job." This attitude firmly maintained will, in the long run, prove best for all concerned.

1. *Specific Persons Are Involved*

For whom should the officers and teachers' meeting be designed? In the planning of the meeting, provision should be made for every teacher and department or general officer who has responsibility for any part of the work in the Sunday school.

The leaders who plan the program of the meeting should answer fully and satisfactorily these questions: What is being provided for Cradle Roll and Nursery workers? What will be helpful for those who work with the Beginner children? What will make it worth while for workers with the Primaries? Will the needs of workers with Juniors be met? Will officers and teachers working with Intermediates find help for their problems? How can those who serve Young People be aided to do a better job? What practical service can be rendered to those responsible for the teaching of Adults? How can Extension workers be benefited? What account will be taken of the secretaries, musicians, and general officers? If the interests and needs of any person or persons belonging to any of these groups are not included, in effect it is being said, "This does not mean you!"

2. Specific Purposes and Procedures Are Proposed

In a certain church, following the fellowship meal and the period of announcements and promotion, all those present were called on to listen to the teaching of the Uniform Lesson for the next Sunday. This plan had been proposed and voted by the officers and teachers themselves. The claim was that the best available teacher could be secured to "teach the lesson," thus giving an example of good teaching and offering broader opportunity for Bible study to those who used the closely Graded Lessons.

The idea seemed attractive, the lesson was usually well presented and enjoyed. Yet the plan was soon recognized as inadequate. A check on attendance disclosed that officers and teachers of Intermediate grades and below had quit coming, since the meeting gave them no specific help; teachers of Young People and Adults frankly found their interest flagging, since the teaching of the lesson, no matter how expertly done, did not carry over into sufficient help for their classes.

A pastor, seeing that "teaching the lesson" was failing in his situation, decided to major in the officers and teachers' meeting on fellowship and prayer. Following the meal and the general period of announcements and promotion, the hour was given to introductions, to news about the church family, to the welcoming of new church members, to recognition of exceptional records and achievements, to the giving out of cards for visitation, and to presentation of objects of prayer. After Scripture reading and a brief devotional talk by the pastor, the remaining time was devoted to praise and prayer.

For a while gratifying attendance was maintained, but gradually the gathering lost its character as an officers and teachers' meeting, with consequent loss to the Sunday school's growth and effectiveness. There was insufficient identification of the meeting with those expected to attend.

Experience clearly proves that the meeting must provide

specific values for specific persons. Unquestionably this calls for time and thought given to careful and detailed planning. Unwillingness to pay this price will jeopardize the success of any important undertaking. Business and professional men know this to be true and act accordingly. When failures occur they can almost always be traced to violation of this principle of attention to details and of concern to meet the needs of persons. The Sunday school enterprise is no exception. Indeed, religion is so intensely personal that to deal in generalities is to miss the purpose of the church in its service of persons as Christ's representatives.

V. Time and Schedule Should Be Considered

"Dost thou love life? Then do not squander time, for time is the stuff that life is made of." So said Benjamin Franklin and so we all agree. Time is life's other name. What we do with our time determines what we accomplish and who we are. With the increase of other interests and demands, there has been no increase in time by so much as a single second.

Since we cannot expand time, we must conserve it. This fact reminds us of the admonition of Christ: "Seek ye first the kingdom of God, and his righteousness" (Matt. 6:33). There is perhaps no area of life today in which it is more difficult or important to obey this command than in the use of our time.

1. *The Schedule Is Related to the Prayer Meeting*

When shall the officers and teachers' meeting be held? Many years ago churches came to recognize that the spiritual life of the members could not best be developed without a meeting for fellowship and prayer between one Sunday and the next. Wednesday, the mid-point of the week, was almost universally adopted as the day for the prayer service. Since Wednesday is a work day, the accepted time for the meeting was the evening hour.

The weekly officers and teachers' meeting is in reality an extension of the older meeting for fellowship, conference, and prayer. In no sense is it a competitor of the prayer meeting; rather, it is an enlargement and reinforcement.

Confession must be made that the "old-fashioned prayer meeting" has become increasingly difficult to maintain. Yielding to the pressure of demands on their time, the great majority of the average congregation have dropped the prayer meeting out of their lives. The smallness of attendance on this vital church meeting has been the near despair of many pastors and their "inner circles," for they have clearly perceived that in this meeting is to be found the secret of power for the Sunday services and the church's total program.

Recovery of the prayer meeting is closely related to the success of the officers and teachers' meeting. The principle of definite supply for the specific needs of particular individuals and groups is applied through the officers and teachers' meeting to the prayer service also. Those who come in the first hour to share their problems and needs remain in the second hour to seek the source of power for their difficulties and problems through concert of prayer. Again and again, because of this revitalizing of the prayer service, it has become necessary to move into the auditorium to accommodate the crowd.

2. The Schedule Considers Local Conditions

Obviously, scheduling of the weekly officers and teachers' meeting must be considered in the light of local conditions. The fellowship meal has often been found a convenience and attraction not only for those who must come immediately from their work to the church, but also for those who would find it difficult to prepare a meal at home and then reach the church on time. To many the meal affords the delightful privilege of fellowship about the table which would otherwise be denied. In some cases the fellowship meal may be impracticable and a burden, and will, of course, be omitted.

Apart from the meal, there are generally two main periods of the meeting—a general period for reports, announcements, special emphases, inspiration, and promotion; and a period of conferences by departments or age groups. The first part of the department conferences is devoted to promotional matters, the second part to the improvement of teaching. In a subsequent chapter, a variety of schedules will be given.

VI. DIFFICULTIES OF ATTENDANCE SHOULD BE CONFRONTED

If there were not difficulties, there would be no need of planning. Difficulties are the lot of all living things. The seed sown in the ground must survive the difficulties of germination, of sprouting, of growth, and of fruitage. The fish of the water and the birds of the air must survive the dangers of the elements and the attacks of enemies. The higher in the scale of life, the greater are the difficulties to be surmounted.

1. *Difficulties of Nonattendance Must Be Faced*

Of course there are difficulties in the way of a successful officers and teachers' meeting, since it is a living thing! For its inauguration, as we have seen, there must be careful, prayerful, co-operative planning. As the enterprise grows, new problems and difficulties will arise. So far as possible, they should be anticipated, for "forewarned is forearmed." Let us frankly consider some of the almost inevitable difficulties.

Nearly always there are some officers and teachers who will be prevented by unavoidable circumstances from attending the meeting. Shall they therefore be considered ineligible for service in the Sunday school? This is a question which should be settled by the church as it thoughtfully and prayerfully adopts its policy concerning requirements for its Sunday school workers.

Perhaps few churches would be willing to adopt a regulation which would, without exception, exclude from service anyone who cannot or will not attend with reasonable faithfulness the weekly meeting. Yet the difficulties will be multiplied if the church takes no position at all, making it purely a question of personal choice. Nominating committees might well be instructed to give preference to those who agree to attend the weekly officers and teachers' meeting, with discre-

tionary power to nominate others if the circumstances seem
to warrant.

2. *Difficulties of Irregular Attendance Can Be Met*

Then there are officers and teachers whose attendance
will be irregular, sometimes of necessity, sometimes otherwise. What can be done to encourage faithful and regular
attendance? The answer lies in the "persuasive power of personal responsibility." Officers and teachers who are regularly
given a share of personal responsibility for the meeting can
usually be counted on to attend. True, irregularity of attendance may sometimes be a symptom of carelessness and inef-
ficiency in performance of the duties of an office. In this
case, a friendly, personal interview by the pastor, minister of
education, superintendent, or by another teacher may get
the difficulty out in the open and correct it.

Occasionally there is a competent, trained officer or
teacher who does not feel the need of the help offered by
the meeting. As has already been suggested, such a person
needs to be impressed with the privilege and the obligation
to share superior advantage with those less privileged.

Some officers and teachers may have transportation difficulties. Frequently a "share-the-ride" plan can be worked
out so that those with cars may pick up those without cars.
To avoid undue expense or conflicting demands for the use
of any one car, members may alternate with one another in
providing the ride.

VII. PRACTICAL PROBLEMS CAN BE SOLVED

Each situation has its own problems, yet all can be solved
if the leaders are willing to pay the price. We consider here
some problems frequently raised.

1. *Problems of the Fellowship Meal Can Be Solved*

The fellowship meal may be considered desirable or even
necessary, but its preparation and serving may involve difficulties. Care should be taken not to make this a burdensome
chore for a few faithful workers. Care also should be exer-

cised to make the meal wholesome and well balanced, attractive without being expensive, with as little waste as possible.

In the larger church, the answer has often been found in the employed hostess, who buys the food economically, supervises its preparation and serving, and arranges for volunteer help through rotation of departments and classes. If kitchen facilities are lacking, certain departments and classes in turn may bring "covered dishes" which can be quickly and easily served. It has been generally found best to make a moderate charge for the meal, the church providing in its budget for a supplement to care for expenses above the actual cost of food.

What shall be done when father or mother or both are involved in the officers and teachers' meeting, but there are children who cannot be left at home? What provision shall be made for other members of the family who may wish to attend the fellowship meal, but who are not included in the officers and teachers' meeting which follows?

If at all possible, Nursery children should be permitted to go to the same rooms in which they meet for Sunday school. *Church Nursery Guide* is the quarterly periodical prepared to give guidance to those who teach Nursery children on Sundays or weekdays.

For the older children, missionary education may be provided through meetings of the Sunbeams, Girls' Auxiliaries, and Royal Ambassadors, provided this plan is practical in the local situation without taking Sunday school workers out of their meeting.

Many churches promote study groups for young people and adults who attend the Wednesday night meetings, but who are not Sunday school officers or teachers. These study groups may be planned to meet the needs of class officers, to furnish training for prospective Sunday school workers, or to provide classes for the study of training course books on the Bible, doctrines, evangelism, or other matters of general interest. Of course no meeting should ever be scheduled for the Wednesday night period which will take Sunday school workers out of the weekly officers and teachers' meeting.

2. *Problems of Leadership and Opposition Can Be Solved*

How may we meet the objection that the church lacks adequate leadership for the conduct of the meeting? The same leaders who are entrusted with the Sunday school departments and classes can be trusted to give leadership to the meeting of officers and teachers. Much of the remainder of this book will be devoted to plans which can be carried out by any average group of Sunday school officers and teachers.

Suppose there is opposition on the part of certain influential persons in the church? Certainly there should be utmost consideration of their opposition. It should not be met with impatience and intolerance, but rather with sympathetic understanding and persuasive enlightenment. There may be groundless prejudice, honest misunderstanding, personal problems, unfortunate past experience, lack of faith, attachment to tradition. Whatever the reason, let it be brought out into the open and prayerfully and lovingly considered. Yet, if after all has been done to overcome objection, it still remains on the part of the stubborn few, then the welfare and will of the majority should not be defeated, but the church should go ahead quietly and firmly on the principle of the greatest good for the greatest number.

It is suggested that this book BUILDING A BETTER SUNDAY SCHOOL THROUGH THE WEEKLY OFFICERS AND TEACHERS' MEETING will furnish an effective tool in initiating the weekly officers and teachers' meeting. In a church where no such meeting has been held, the first step in actually starting one may be to schedule a study of this book in a class, meeting every Wednesday evening. The study may be scheduled for one hour each week over the period to cover one quarter. It may be correlated with workshop activities based on suggestions in this textbook.

If the class meets at an hour preceding the Wednesday night prayer service, this schedule will help workers to form the habit of coming at the proper time for a weekly officers and teachers' meeting. The study of the book, in an atmosphere of free discussion and prayerful dependence on divine wisdom, will do much to dissolve the opposition of any persons who have lacked information.

Such a study, carried out over the period of one quarter in the program of the Sunday school, should result in specific plans for maintaining a weekly officers and teachers' meeting in line with the suggestions in this book. These plans will be tailor-made to fit the local situation, since they will have come out of the prayerful study by the workers of their own needs and problems and out of the prayerful evaluation of the ideas set forth in this textbook.

Plans having been made, the cost having been counted, what practical procedures shall be followed in order to assure that the weekly officers and teachers' meetings will result in building a better Sunday school? This is the question to be discussed in subsequent chapters.

VIII. THE CHAPTER SUMMARIZED

1. The church should be led to establish the weekly officers and teachers' meeting. This meeting, like the whole Sunday school, should exist by the authority and under the direction of the church.

2. Officers and teachers should be convinced of the need. The success of the meeting depends on the extent to which it supplies the needs of those who attend.

3. The purpose of the meeting should be clarified. It must not be just another meeting, but a coming together for the achievement of worthy and clearly defined objectives.

4. Persons expected to attend should be identified. It is not a general, optional meeting but a conference of specified persons with defined responsibilities.

5. Time and schedule should be considered. The meeting should conserve time and be arranged to meet the convenience of the majority.

6. Difficulties of attendance should be confronted. While the obligation to attend should be recognized and accepted by all, arbitrary demands should be avoided.

7. Practical problems can be solved. Details as to the conduct and leadership of the meeting may present difficulties, but they are never insuperable.

CHAPTER 4

4

The Weekly Officers and
Teachers' Meeting Insures Better
Administration and Promotion

IN FULFILLING its teaching ministry, a church operates as a
school. Its complex organization and varied activities call
for sound administration. Its plans to reach and teach all
available persons must be effectively promoted. Administration and promotion are not incidental but fundamental to
the success of the Sunday school.

It is difficult to make sharp separation between the functions of administration and promotion and the work of teaching. Some of the most important lessons taught by the Sunday
school come through the experiences of the members as they
work together in the efficient conduct of the school and in
the broadening of its outreach. The purpose of this chapter
is to show how the administrative and promotional phases
of the Sunday school can best be dealt with through the
weekly meeting of officers and teachers.

I. THE SUNDAY SCHOOL REQUIRES EFFICIENT ADMINISTRATION

The general superintendent is the Sunday school's chief
administrative officer. He is chosen by the church to lead in
administering the affairs of the school. His ability will be
tested not so much by what he himself does as by his ability
to find, guide, and inspire others who will do the work well.
He should feel a deep sense of responsibility for the smooth
and efficient operation of each aspect of the life of the school.
He stands alongside the pastor and the minister of education

45

(if any) as a commissioned and dedicated servant of Christ and of the church.

1. The Importance of Administration Should Be Realized

To minister is to serve. A church exists to serve, not to be served. Teaching and preaching are not ends in themselves but means of ministry by which the lost are won to Christ and the saved are enlisted in his service. The Sunday school could not be a teaching agency without also being a service agency.

To administer is to serve with a purpose, or to provide ways and means by which service can be made effective. To minister without administration would be much like using a tool without a handle. The more important the enterprise, the greater necessity there is for efficient administration. Too often the lack of sound administration weakens the teaching ministry of the church and thus limits its usefulness.

2. The Need of Administration Should Be Supplied

What is administration? Ordway Tead, an authority in the field of business administration, says: "Administration is conceived as the necessary activities of those individuals (executives) in an organization who are charged with ordering, forwarding, and facilitating the associated efforts of a group of individuals brought together to realize certain defined purposes." *

Translated into terms of the Sunday school, administration is the responsibility of the church-elected officers—particularly the general superintendent and the department superintendents—to organize, systematize, inform and inspire, guide and direct the energies and abilities of all those associated in the church program of teaching and learning. That this may be done efficiently calls for intelligence and consecration.

With earnest prayerfulness a church, under the pastor's leadership, should discover and develop the most capable

* By permission from The Art of Administration, by Ordway Tead. Copyright 1951. McGraw-Hill Book Company, Inc. pp. 3-4.

persons in its membership as administrative leaders of the various organizations. Together, the administrative leaders of the Sunday school should furnish as efficient administration for the school of the church as would be expected of the administrators of the public schools, the businesses and industries, or the public and private institutions of the community. It is difficult for a school to lift the level of teaching above the level of administration.

II. THE SUNDAY SCHOOL NEEDS CONTINUOUS PROMOTION

The administrative duties of the general superintendent include promotion. He of course is not solely responsible, but if he does not lead out, the promotional aspect of the Sunday school will usually lag and the school will consequently fail to grow.

In a department school administrative duties likewise fall upon the department superintendents. They have chief responsibility for promoting and maintaining a high average of attendance of the department officers and teachers at all workers' meetings as well as Sunday sessions. When an absence from the weekly officers and teachers' meeting occurs, the superintendent should at once find out the reason. If an officer or teacher begins to lose interest or to become irregular or to find fault, the superintendent should investigate and, through a personal conference, seek to correct the difficulty.

In the department sessions of the weekly officers and teachers' meetings, the department superintendents have practically the same functions as the general superintendent has in the general sessions.

1. *Promotion Is Not Optional*

To promote is to set forward. The only direction in which a moving object will run without being propelled is downhill. The locomotive must be refueled, the automobile gas tank must be refilled, we ourselves must replenish energy with food. A Sunday school cannot simply be provided with a place to meet, with officers and teachers, and then be expected to go forward without promotion. So swift is the pace, so rapid the changes, so severe the competition for the time and energy of the people today, that a Sunday school cannot stand still without going backward.

2. *Promotion Calls for Qualified Persons*

Promotion, like administration, calls for the best thought and ability which the church can afford. No one promotional plan will suffice—there must be continuous creative planning. Left to a "convenient" time, made dependent on impulse and occasional concern, promotion will be weak and ineffective and the progress of the church will be hindered. Just as preaching and teaching demand week-by-week study and prayer, so should promotion be the object of continuous, prayerful thought and planning.

III. ADMINISTRATION AND PROMOTION REQUIRE CO-OPERATION

To co-operate is to think and work together. Administration and promotion cannot be carried on at a desk. The pastor, minister of education, or general superintendent may sit in seclusion and devise plans for carrying on and enlarging the work of the Sunday school, but ideas on paper must be communicated to fellow workers and put into operation jointly. Announcements, descriptions, arguments, and exhortations will not suffice. Group-mindedness is needed, so that the plans become not "his" or "theirs" but "ours."

1. *Co-operation Necessitates Shared Responsibilities*

The heart of administration and promotion is division of labor and responsibility. Nobody can do everything, nor can everybody do everything equally well. Nothing would be done at all if everybody waited until he could do it so perfectly that nobody could find fault with it! The democratic process calls for the sharing of disagreements as well as agreements. "In the multitude of counsellors there is safety" (Prov. 11:14). Many excellent plans fail because they are individually rather than collectively conceived and projected. Nowhere more than in a group of Baptists is there necessity for collective planning and deciding, if desired results are to be achieved. The very genius of our Baptist church life calls for co-operation in administration and promotion.

2. Co-operation Is Gained Through the Superintendent's Cabinet and Monthly Workers' Council

An effective weekly officers and teachers' meeting depends largely upon the functioning of the general superintendent's cabinet. This conference brings together the administrative officers of the Sunday school, particularly the pastor, minister of education, general superintendent, associate superintendents, general secretary and associate secretary, and the department superintendents.

In most churches the cabinet meets monthly. The general superintendent, who is in charge of the meeting, has one of his best opportunities to exercise creative administration as he leads the group to deal with special problems, construct the calendar of activities, attend to questions of correlation, project plans for improvement and enlargement, suggest new and better ways of conducting the officers and teachers' meeting, concentrate attention on timely events, prepare recommendations to the church, and deal with other matters related to the local situation. Details of administration and promotion can be worked out first in the cabinet meeting, thus conserving time in the regular officers and teachers' meeting. Where feasible, a weekly meeting of the cabinet will prove valuable.

One of the regular weekly officers and teachers' meetings each month may be designated as the monthly workers' conference. At this meeting, in the general period and in the department periods, written reports for the past month will be submitted and checks made on the goals and achievements. The plans for the month which have been worked out in the superintendent's cabinet will be presented to the entire group of workers for their consideration and adoption.

IV. Time Is Needed for Inspiration

Just as preaching and teaching are more effective in an

atmosphere made warm through worship, so administration and promotion need the aid of inspiration.

1. *Inspiration May Be Misinterpreted*

By *inspiration* is not meant an artificial pumping up of enthusiasm. Noisy "pep talks" and boisterous "boosting" are not to be confused with inspiration. To inspire is literally to breathe into, as when Jesus "breathed on them [the disciples], and saith unto them, Receive ye the Holy Ghost" (John 20:22). In the human sense, to inspire is to present ideas so that they animate, enliven, exhilarate, encourage, incite to action.

2. *Inspiration Must Be Intelligently Provided*

How can such an inspiring atmosphere be created and maintained?

First, inspiration is gained by claiming the promise of Christ, "For where two or three are gathered together in my name, there am I in the midst of them" (Matt. 18:20). The "two or three" may be twenty or thirty or two hundred or three hundred; the condition is that they be gathered "in his name." Whatever plans are proposed should therefore be as in the Master's presence and with his approval. To ask, "Lord, what wilt thou have us to do?" will both clear up the atmosphere and charge it with power.

Second, inspiration comes when the guidance of the Holy Spirit is sought. Jesus promised that "when he, the Spirit of truth, is come, he will guide you into all truth" (John 16:13). Prayer for guidance will be answered. This does not mean that we are to wait idly and passively for the Holy Spirit to tell us what to do. God has given us minds which he expects us to use, but he has also given us the Holy Spirit to illumine our minds and to give us guidance as we do our part.

Third, inspiration results from the challenge of the difficult and the promise of success. Jesus also promised: "In the world ye shall have tribulation [pressure, trouble, difficulty]; but be of good cheer; I have overcome the world" (John 16:33). Easy tasks are seldom inspiring and "work without hope draws water in a sieve." Put together the challenging and the possible, confront the difficult with the achievable, and the human spirit will rise to higher levels of determination and action. Paul was thus inspired when, facing the humanly impossible, he declared, "I can do all things through Christ which strengtheneth me" (Phil. 4:13).

Fourth, inspiration comes from fellowship. Singly, we see the discouragements and the prospects of failure. Together, we realize that the obstacles can be overcome. According to the divine arithmetic, "Five of you shall chase an hundred, and an hundred of you shall put ten thousand to flight" (Lev. 26:8). A new spirit is infused into the individual by the group when "I-ness" is replaced by "we-ness." Around the table during the fellowship meal and in the first moments of the general period of the officers and teachers' meeting, the element of inspiration should be sought and found.

V. Time Is Needed for Information

1. *Information Is the Basis of Achievement*

Information is essential to achievement. The general superintendent should be careful to see that adequate information has been prepared for the meeting. The uninformed Sunday school officer or teacher is somewhat like the driver on a crowded highway at night whose automobile lights are out. He will either drive off on the side of the road and stop or he will risk collision by driving on. The normal course would be just to get out of the way.

Is not this the picture of the Sunday school worker who does not know what is going on? Since his lack of information is liable to cause him to be a troublemaker, he steps aside and lets those who are better informed "run the church." It is difficult to say who are the greater stumbling blocks, the uninformed troublemakers or the uninformed shirkers. Ordinarily the latter constitute the majority. Their case is hopeful, for their needed information and training can be readily supplied.

Time should always be provided in the officers and teach-

SCHOOL REPORT

SUNDAY_____19____

CLASS OR DEPARTMENT	Enrolled	Memb. Present	New Memb.	Visitors	Total Present	On Time	Bibles Bro't	Contributing	Prep'd Lessons	Att'g Pr'ch'g	Amount Offering	Grade
General Officers												
Totals Today												
Extension												
Cradle Roll												
Total Enrolment												
Totals Last Sunday												

100% Members_____ Visits Made_____ Phone Calls_____ Letters & Cards_____ Total Contacts_____

Comments_____

FORM 70S. SIX POINT RECORD SYSTEM. BROADMAN SUPPLIES. NASHVILLE, TENNESSEE

This form has information for study in the general promotional period. If a longer form is needed, use 70 L. Forms 425S or 425 L are similar.

DEPARTMENT REPORT

DEPARTMENT_____SUNDAY_____19____

CLASS	Enrolled	Memb. Present	New Memb.	Visitors	Total Present	On Time	Bibles Bro't	Contributing	Prep'd Lessons	Att'g Pr'ch'g	Amount Offering	Grade
Department Officers												
Totals												

100% Members_____ Visits Made_____ Phone Calls_____ Letters & Cards_____ Total Contacts_____

FORM 42S. SIX POINT RECORD SYSTEM. BROADMAN SUPPLIES. NASHVILLE, TENNESSEE

This form is used for study in the departments. Special forms are available for Cradle Roll and Extension departments, which keep formal records on a monthly basis. Form 420S is similar.

ers' meeting for securing and for giving interesting and help-ful information.

2. *Information Should Be Accurate and Challenging*

Reports which interpret last Sunday's record should be made and studied. The detailed reports may be mimeo-graphed or displayed on a chalkboard. A mere array of fig-ures, however, will be largely meaningless. Significant facts should be highlighted—comparison made of totals with last Sunday, a month ago, a year ago; high points and low points spotlighted; recognition given to exceptional departments and classes; weaknesses indicated that need strengthening. The forms provided in the Six Point Record System are de-signed to facilitate the preparation and study of the reports.

Announcements should be briefly and attractively made. The announcements may include the pastor's word concern-ing the church plans, statements of interest from other church organizations, information as to coming events, noteworthy news, proposed projects, emphasized events in the calendar of activities, and the like. Again, time will be saved and the announcements better remembered if they are mimeographed or written on the chalkboard.

VI. Time Is Needed for Promotional Matters

The general superintendent is always concerned for effi-cient organization. Organization means the relating of each part to every other part and to the whole so as to prevent waste and friction and to achieve the best results in the shortest time.

1. *Organizational Matters Should Be Listed*

Time may not be needed at every meeting of the officers and teachers for organizational matters. Yet frequently such matters as the following should be considered:

Beginning and closing on time
Relation of the assembly period to the teaching period
The classification of new members
The taking and reporting of the records

The protection of classes from interruptions and distractions

The maintenance of reverence and good order

Planned visitation of prospects and absentees

Concern for attendance on and behavior in the worship services

Review of the Standards

Co-operation in the church plans for evangelism, stewardship, missions

Since only a few minutes can be devoted to organizational matters, careful planning in the superintendent's cabinet is a prerequisite to effective promotion in the weekly officers and teachers' meeting. It is well to make a list of matters such as the foregoing which will need attention and then place each of the interests on the calendar so that it will be emphasized at the proper time—none overstressed and none neglected.

2. *Goals Should Be Set and Achievements Studied*

Attention should be given to enlargement. Enrolment and attendance goals should be set, visitation of prospects and absentees planned, the farther outreach of the church and Sunday school considered, from "Jerusalem . . . unto the uttermost part."

Achievements should be publicized. Workers need to know what is being accomplished in reaching, teaching, winning, enlisting more people for Christ and the church through the Sunday school. Care should be taken not to prolong this period of information, and every available means should be used to present the information visually and attractively.

VII. TIME IS NEEDED FOR CONCENTRATION

No one should realize more keenly than the general superintendent the preciousness of time. The limitations of the Sunday school call for a high degree of concentration. Whereas the public school has its pupils five days a week and six hours a day, the Sunday school has its pupils one day a week and an hour and a half a day (except for the extended session in Nursery departments). Since we believe that Christian education is even more important than secular education, we must make utmost use of the time for Bible study. We must employ the principle of processors of foods, who eliminate unnecessary weight and bulk while retaining essential values.

1. Concentration Calls for a Calendar

Concentration will be needed in the officers and teachers' meeting. A calendar of emphases may be prepared which will spotlight certain interests and activities in line with the denominational Calendar of Activities and the calendar of the church itself. Of course each annual calendar will vary according to the special emphases needed. Usually the following items will be among those included:

(1) *Winter.*—Major on Bible study and missions, including: Convention-wide January Bible Study Week, daily Bible reading and home study, biblical and doctrinal training course books, improvement of Bible teaching methods, examination and analysis of curriculum materials, associational Vacation Bible school clinics, churchwide study course week sponsored by the Training Union in March, home missions emphasis, school of missions, observance of Home Missions Day in the Sunday school, discovery and enlistment of new workers, studies in soul-winning, and preparation for special season of evangelism.

(2) *Spring.*—Let the emphases include: churchwide evangelism with the Sunday school effectively utilized, conservation of evangelistic results by enlistment of new members in the Sunday school, Christian Home Week, special programs on the home and church working together, Life Commitment Day, Extension Department Day, Vacation Bible schools in the mother church and in mission points, home visitation, welcome to returning students, study of church rolls to discover leadership prospects.

(3) *Summer.*—Provide for: Youth Week and youth revival, special recreation and fellowship features, attendance

on Convention-wide and state summer assemblies, religious census, stress on duties of nominating committee, review of building and equipment needs, publicizing the association calendar, Preparation Week, Harvest Day, plans for Promotion Day, expanding the organization for growth during the new Sunday school year.

(4) *Fall.*—Deal with: co-operation in Training Union enlargement, installation of officers and teachers, checking achievements against the Standards, intensified soul-winning, stewardship and church financing according to the church plan, State Mission Day, Harvest Day in the Sunday school, Thanksgiving and Christmas observances, child care ministries (Orphanage Day in the Sunday school), foreign missions and the Lottie Moon Christmas offering.

2. *The Calendar May Be Varied to Meet Conditions*

The calendar adopted by the church will vary from year to year according to the Convention-wide denominational calendar and the Sunday school calendar which is proposed by the state Sunday school department and the Sunday School Department of the Baptist Sunday School Board. This Sunday school calendar is clearly outlined each fall in the planning booklet issued by the Sunday School Department of the Baptist Sunday School Board, and used as a guide during Preparation Week in the churches. *The Sunday School Builder* will prove a constant source of guidance in promoting the items in the calendar of Sunday school activities.

With all the matters located on the calendar, a further breakdown may be made as each emphasis or event is given its proper place on the week of the month where it belongs. When printed or mimeographed and made available, the calendar automatically brings up the interest or activity to be spotlighted.

VIII. Time Is Needed for Mobilization

To mobilize is to make ready for active service. It is not enough to inspire, inform, organize, and concentrate. The test comes with what happens afterward—especially on Sunday. The words of Paul apply after any Spirit-directed planning: "Now therefore perform the doing of it; that as there was a readiness to will, so there may be a performance also" (2 Cor. 8:11). Jesus demands that we go beyond understanding and assenting: "If ye know these things, happy are ye if ye do them" (John 13:17).

1. Total Mobilization Is the Ideal

The high point of the officers and teachers' meeting is reached with "total mobilization of total ability for total achievement of a unanimously accepted goal." * Breaking this ideal down into its several parts, we have:

(1) *Total mobilization*—the wholehearted readiness of every member of the group to act together in carrying out what has been proposed and decided

(2) *Total ability*—each in his or her place bringing to the service of the undertaking all skills and powers of body, mind, and soul

(3) *For total achievement*—no stopping short, no falling back, no excuses for unfinished tasks, but the finishing of the job with complete detail and in full measure

(4) *Of a unanimously accepted goal*—no grumbling or complaining, no withdrawals or reservations, but complete agreement as to the wisdom and the worthiness of the objective, counting no sacrifices too great for its attainment

2. Progressive Mobilization May Be Achieved

Perhaps such an ideal sounds visionary when we think of real persons in a given church. Yet would any less ideal be pleasing to Christ? Nothing less than this ideal would have satisfied Paul, who said: "I count all things but loss for the excellency of the knowledge of Christ Jesus my Lord." "Brethren, I count not myself to have apprehended: but this one thing I do, forgetting those things which are behind, and reaching forth unto those things which are before, I press toward the mark for the prize of the high calling of God in

* Ordway Tead, *Ibid.*, p. 33.

Christ Jesus" (Phil. 3:8, 13–14). He then summons all who are like-minded to imitate his example.

Would it not be a serious charge against us as officers and teachers of the school in which the highest ideals of conduct are taught and sought if we ourselves attempted no great things for God? We are bound to conclude that the weekly officers and teachers' meeting would prove ultimately a failure if it did not mobilize resources for the doing of God's will as it has been disclosed through prayerful discussion of needs to be met. Jesus himself stated the test: "If ye keep my commandments, ye shall abide in my love; even as I have kept my Father's commandments, and abide in his love." "Ye are my friends, if ye do whatsoever I command you" (John 15:10, 14).

IX. The Brevity of Time Requires Conservation

1. A Typical Schedule Is Suggested

A survey of some three hundred officers and teachers' meetings disclosed the following typical schedule:

FELLOWSHIP MEAL (30 minutes)
May be omitted in some cases.

GENERAL PROMOTIONAL PERIOD (15 minutes)

DEPARTMENT CONFERENCES (15 minutes)
In class schools, combine with general period.

TEACHING IMPROVEMENT PERIODS (45 minutes)
Although many schedules allow only 30 minutes, experience shows that 45 minutes are needed for best results.

PRAYER MEETING

2. A Warning as to Timing Is Needed

While some administrative and promotional details can be cared for during the meal, most of these matters must be compressed into fifteen minutes. To take longer is to jeopardize the department meetings, particularly that period which is the heart of it all—the period for improvement of teaching. We may well take a lesson from those who arrange radio and television programs, most of which are limited to fifteen minutes. It is still true that "the king's business required haste" (1 Sam. 21:8). This reminder should ever confront those who plan and preside over the administrative and promotional period of the weekly officers and teachers' meeting.

X. THE CHAPTER SUMMARIZED

1. The Sunday school requires efficient administration. Sound administration is essential to successful teaching; hence the necessity to discover and develop capable administrative officers.

2. The Sunday school needs continuous promotion. Promotion, likewise essential to teaching, calls for prayer, thought, and planning.

3. Administration and promotion require co-operation. Co-operation, also indispensable to successful teaching, is necessary for collective planning and deciding.

4. Time is needed for inspiration. The meeting should include something that enlivens, exhilarates, encourages, and incites to action.

5. Time is needed for information. The meeting affords opportunity to keep the whole church informed about the whole program.

6. Time is needed for promotional matters. Matters of organization must be given attention faithfully and regularly.

7. Time is needed for concentration. Since many matters must be given attention in minimum time, plans should be made that will focus attention upon a well-planned calendar of activities.

8. Time is needed for mobilization. The officers and teachers' meeting seeks "total mobilization of total ability for total achievement of a unanimously accepted goal."

9. The brevity of time requires conservation. The schedule should be so arranged as to conserve time and include all important matters.

CHAPTER 5

I. BETTER TEACHING CALLS FOR BETTER TEACHERS
   1. The Teacher's Personality Is Pre-eminently Important
   2. Personality Is Enriched Through Group Study

II. BETTER TEACHING REQUIRES BIBLE KNOWLEDGE
   1. Teaching Comes from the Overflow
   2. Knowledge Comes Through the Meeting

III. BETTER TEACHING REQUIRES PUPIL STUDY
   1. Knowing the Pupils Is Highly Important
   2. The Workers' Meeting Implements Pupil Study

IV. BETTER TEACHING REQUIRES UNDERSTANDING OF TEACHING
   1. The Meaning of Teaching Needs Clarification
   2. The Meaning of Teaching Should Be Discussed

V. BETTER TEACHING REQUIRES CLARITY OF AIMS
   1. Aims Need Clear Definition
   2. Plans are Needed for Studying Aims

VI. BETTER TEACHING REQUIRES USE OF RESOURCES
   1. The Wealth of Helps Should Be Disclosed
   2. Skill in Using Helps Should Be Developed

VII. BETTER TEACHING REQUIRES FAVORABLE CONDITIONS
   1. Investigate Conditions that Affect Teaching
   2. Helpful Discussions Should Follow the Investigations

VIII. BETTER TEACHING REQUIRES EVALUATION OF RESULTS
   1. Results Should Be Tested
   2. Outcomes of Tests Should Be Discussed

IX. SCHEDULING A PROGRAM OF IMPROVEMENT
   1. A Program of Systematic Improvement Is Needed
   2. A Schedule by Quarters Is Suggested

X. THE CHAPTER SUMMARIZED

5

The Weekly Officers and Teachers' Meeting Improves Teaching

"WHAT IS the biggest room in your new educational building?" a pastor was asked. "The room for improvement!" he replied. If the question were pressed further, "Specifically, what improvement?" the almost unanimous response would be, "The improvement of teaching."

Although improvements are needed in building and equipment, in organization, in curriculum, in enrichment materials, in visitation and enlargement, in enlistment and stewardship, in evangelism and missions—the paramount need is that of effective, fruitful teaching. The weekly officers and teachers' meeting can make its greatest contribution through the improvement of teaching.

I. BETTER TEACHING CALLS FOR BETTER TEACHERS

What is education? Arthur Guiterman says:

> For Education is, Making Men;
> So is it now, so was it when
> Mark Hopkins sat on one end of the log
> And James Garfield sat on the other.

1. *The Teacher's Personality Is Pre-eminently Important*

A teacher with a class of one may change not only that life but the lives of many others. Anne Mansfield Sullivan dedicated her life to the teaching of a blind deaf-mute, but that girl was Helen Keller, whose life has blessed multitudes. Jesus devoted more of his time to teaching twelve men than to any other single activity during his redemptive ministry. For most of us, the teacher is more significant than the les-

61

son, for only through the teacher does the lesson become meaningful.

2. Personality Is Enriched Through Group Study

The first aim of the teaching improvement period should be the enrichment of the personality of officers and teachers. This can be accomplished in several ways.

"Know yourself" said the philosopher Socrates. Self-examination is often the first step toward self-improvement. A brief period in each of a series of meetings may be devoted to discussion of one or more of such questions as the following:

What are the essential qualifications of Sunday school officers and teachers?

What obligations did we assume when we were elected?

How can we maintain maximum physical health?

How can we keep mentally alert?

How can we keep our social lives wholesome?

How can we deepen our spiritual lives? Workers, even those in the Nursery departments, may consider the question: What truths in this current unit of lessons will contribute to my personal enrichment?

In the course of a quarter, lives may be transformed and thus fitted more perfectly to be vessels "unto honour, sanctified, and meet for the master's use, and prepared unto every good work" (2 Tim. 2:21).

II. BETTER TEACHING REQUIRES BIBLE KNOWLEDGE

To "know yourself," must be added "know your Bible" if teaching is to be satisfying.

1. Teaching Comes from the Overflow

Too often teachers are content to "teach the lesson," meaning the passage or passages of Scripture indicated for immediate study. Results are most gratifying when the teacher "teaches from the overflow," from fulness of knowledge of the Bible as a whole.

It is a truism that the Bible is its own best interpreter. Difficulties in a given passage are often cleared up in the light of related passages. Unfortunate and misleading interpretations can best be avoided by a knowledge of the total context. Baptists have historically based their doctrines on the plain and broad meaning of the Scriptures and this, in large measure, accounts for their theological stability.

2. Knowledge Comes Through the Meeting

The weekly officers and teachers' meeting affords opportunity both to stress the need of Bible study and to make plans to supply the need. Of course not all the Bible and doctrinal study needed can be provided in the brief time of this meeting, but much can be done to stimulate desire for broader Bible knowledge and to arrange for its fulfilment through such activities as the following:

(1) At the beginning of each new series of lessons, "preview studies" may be conducted, giving a brief and comprehensive look at the entire unit. Guidance leaflets may be secured from the Sunday School Department of the Baptist Sunday School Board. The preview should be made in a regular training class outside of the weekly officers and teachers' meeting, or be completed by the individual study plan. In either case, workers should be encouraged to use in each weekly meeting the notes made during the preview study.

(2) At the beginning of a quarter or a unit of lessons, a simple paper and pencil preview test may be given in the weekly meeting, to discover what is or is not known about the lessons ahead—dates, author or authors, principal characters, main events, most important teachings, difficult words and terms, misunderstood doctrines, or other matters of specific knowledge. Guidance should be offered for personal study based on the needs revealed by such a test.

(3) Suggestions may be made by the pastor as to sermons and prayer meeting topics which will relate to a given unit.

(4) Some of the biblical and doctrinal training course books may be circulated to be studied by the individual plan.

(5) From time to time, a week of concentrated study of a selected biblical or doctrinal training course book may be planned and promoted.

(6) Observance of Bible Study Week in January should be made churchwide with effort made to enlist every member in a course which provides for all ages.

(7) Officers and teachers should be enlisted in daily Bible reading—both as outlined in the Sunday school periodicals and as provided by the Training Union—and in participation in Training Union programs.

At times it will be well for the superintendent, or some leader he designates, to use a part of the teaching improvement period to lead the workers in a step-by-step study of a Bible passage. Since the aim will be, first of all, the personal enrichment of the workers, this procedure may be used occasionally for workers with any age group. If a lesson passage is used, the group study by workers with Adults or Young People becomes a demonstration of group study such as the teacher might direct during a class period.

Such activities, followed year by year will produce teaching of a quality vastly superior to that which comes when teachers live "from hand to mouth."

III. BETTER TEACHING REQUIRES PUPIL STUDY

To the instructions: "know yourself" and "know your Bible," must be added "know your pupils."

1. Knowing the Pupils Is Highly Important

The Bible is not a book of abstractions. It is an inspired record and interpretation of the experiences of persons with God and of persons with persons. It came out of experience and is intended to go back into experience. Literally, we do not teach lessons but persons by means of lessons. It is essential therefore that officers and teachers know whom they teach as well as what they teach.

Just as the Bible should be known as a whole, so the total personality of each pupil should be studied. This involves knowing something about the home life, the school or work life, neighborhood and acquaintances, likes and dislikes, leisure time interests and activities, educational level and Bible knowledge, spiritual condition and church relationship, attainments as indicated by averages on the Six Point Record System, and other matters.

A "Pupil's Life History" notebook should be kept, in which will be entered statistical information concerning each class member, with notes made from time to time indicating facts and observations gathered from contacts and study. Sunday school teaching thus becomes an everyday responsibility and reaches from the immediate occasion when the lesson is taught into all important areas of each pupil's life.

2. The Workers' Meeting Implements Pupil Study

The weekly officers and teachers' meeting affords opportunity to develop and to implement this ideal of pupil study. Place should be made in the schedule for stimulating, planning, and directing such study on the part of teachers. Such plans as the following may be used:

(1) Home visitation should be stressed, with an occasional checkup to see if officers and teachers are regularly visiting in the homes of their pupils. This emphasis will be in addition to the regular week-by-week reports and assignments on visitation.

(2) A series of brief discussions of "problem pupils and the problems of pupils" may be arranged. Helpful books may be suggested for personal study.

(3) Problems involving inattention and disorder may be brought up for brief discussion.

(4) Stress may be laid on the opportunity and responsibility of teachers and officers as counselors of pupils who have suffered bereavement, illness, loss or disappointment, wounded feelings, or other forms of distress.

(5) Appropriate filmstrips from the *Know Your Child Series* may be studied. (See *Baptist Book Store Catalog*.)

(6) The pastor may be asked to suggest sermons and prayer meeting subjects which will be helpful in understanding people and meeting their needs.

(7) Training course books, selected because they will help workers understand persons, will of course be circulated and their intensive study promoted.

IV. BETTER TEACHING REQUIRES UNDERSTANDING OF TEACHING

Of great importance to effective teaching is a satisfactory understanding of the process. Some of the most gratifying meetings of officers and teachers may be devoted to this clarification.

1. *The Meaning of Teaching Needs Clarification*

The approach to the problem in the officers and teachers' meeting may well be through the question addressed to each teacher: "What do you do when you teach?" The varied replies may include such methods as: commenting on the lesson verse by verse, asking and answering questions, retelling the lesson in story form, explaining and illustrating the meaning of the lesson, stimulating and guiding discussion, calling for and commenting on assignments previously made, following closely the printed helps, finding answers through use of Bibles, presenting the lesson in lecture fashion, combinations of these and other methods.

2. *The Meaning of Teaching Should Be Discussed*

Such replies as the foregoing set the stage for guided discussion of the question: What is teaching?

A list of questions may be compiled by the workers and placed in their notebooks to direct their study:

What happens when the teacher teaches and the learner learns?

What are necessary procedures in preparing to teach?

How can we overcome temptations to superficial study?

How can we use the available "helps" in preparing to teach?

What books are most helpful toward an understanding of teaching?

What misunderstandings of teaching should be cleared up?

In the teaching improvement periods, over a space of time, the answers may be sought through such procedures as the following:

(1) Workers may share with one another points they have discovered through their study (outside the weekly officers and teachers' meeting) of one of the general or department books on teaching in the Church Study Course.

(2) Workers to whom outside research has been assigned may report on the viewpoints in several of the basic textbooks on teaching in the training course, and lead the group to compare the findings.

(3) Three or four teachers in the group may constitute a panel, each stating his concept of teaching; then members of the group may raise questions.

(4) Occasionally a "resource person"—usually a trained teacher or supervisor who has had successful experience in the educational field—may be brought in to answer questions proposed by the group.

(5) A member of the group may teach a "demonstration lesson" following which there will be a general discussion of the points at which the lesson has demonstrated real teaching.

(6) The nature and methods of teaching may be studied by means of visual aids, such as the five Broadman filmstrips in the "Teacher Improvement Series." (Secure through your nearest Baptist Book Store. See the current *Baptist Book Store Catalog* for descriptions.)

Such an occasional series of discussions and demonstrations may well revolutionize the concept of teaching which some teachers hold and bring permanent enrichment to their teaching. As the study progresses, workers should record in their notebooks their own conclusions and the group consensus in answer to the basic question: What is teaching?

V. Better Teaching Requires Clarity of Aims

What am I teaching for? is an arresting question. All teaching, it may be answered, is of course for results, but the question persists, What results? The results may be those intended and desired, or they may be unintended and undesired. The pupil may learn the memory work and at the same time learn to dislike the Bible. He may learn to appreciate Sunday school but develop an aversion for the preaching service. He may memorize the Ten Commandments but cheat in marking up his record envelope. The teacher may teach Bible truth but the pupil's misunderstanding may turn it into error. The teacher may make the lesson clear but the pupil may see no relation of it to his life. The teacher may have no real aim in teaching, hence the pupil will have no purpose in learning.

1. *Aims Need Clear Definition*

The officers and teachers' meeting gives opportunity for the question to be faced by each teacher: What is my aim in teaching? One may answer, "I aim to teach the Bible"; another, "I aim to win to Christ," or "to develop character"; or another may say, "I aim to impart Christian ideals"; or "I aim to change attitudes." Still another may say, "I aim to secure Christian conduct." Let us agree that there is value in each of these statements. Then let us seek to lead teachers to clarify and unify their aims.

The study of aims may occupy several weeks, and be introduced by having workers propose such questions as:

Why are clearly-defined aims necessary?

How are aims determined?

What are the tests of good aims?

What are the several kinds of aims?

Should we seek knowledge, attitudes, choices, and conduct separately or simultaneously?

What is the relation of aims to methods?

How can we keep aims Bible centered and pupil centered at the same time?

2. *Plans Are Needed for Studying Aims*

The discussion of aims may be carried on in several ways in the teaching improvement periods. No suggested procedure will be equally practical in all situations, but ideas such as the following may be adapted to various age groups:

(1) The general subject of aims in teaching may be lifted

out from basic training course books on teaching and re-examined. From several of these texts, statements as to aims may be compared and reviewed.

(2) More specifically, aims in the appropriate age group book on teaching and department administration may be examined.

(3) A given series or unit of lessons may be investigated, appropriately at the beginning of the study, with a view to determining aims as to knowledge to be acquired, attitudes to be formed, choices to be made, conduct to be sought. Similar investigation may be made at the close of a series or unit, in the effort to determine what aims were achieved.

(4) Various workers may each propose an aim for the current lesson, or group of lessons, and evaluate each aim according to agreed criteria.

(5) A "demonstration lesson" may be taught, following which there may be discussion of the teacher's aims and how successfully they were achieved.

VI. BETTER TEACHING REQUIRES USE OF RESOURCES

True, the poor workman may blame his tools, but the skilled workman will do better work with good tools. To the *what* and *who* and *why* must be added the *how* of teaching.

1. *The Wealth of Helps Should Be Disclosed*

Many good teachers are handicapped by lack of resources. Frequently the only material used in lesson preparation and presentation are the Bible, the teacher's periodical, and the pupil's quarterly or book. In many cases, the pupil's helps are not at hand. Often the teacher is unaware of the wealth of helpful material available. Sunday schools are known to have repeated the same order year after year, apparently unacquainted with new developments in the field of periodical literature, quarterlies, books, and visual aids.

2. *Skill in Using Helps Should Be Developed*

In connection with the study of teaching methods, the weekly officers and teachers' meeting affords excellent opportunity to help teachers become acquainted with the tools provided for their use and to develop skill in using available materials. This study of resources of teaching may include the following:

(1) There may be a period of stock-taking as to what helps are now being used by officers and teachers.

(2) The group may make an examination and appraisal of available periodicals for teachers and officers of the age group, such as the teacher's book, other age group helps, *The Sunday School Builder*, and other supplementary materials, and profit by guided practice in how to use these materials.

(3) There may be an exhibit and appraisal of the annual lesson commentaries in book form, and of the teachers' Bibles, commentaries, concordances, Bible dictionaries, and atlases available in your church library.

(4) The use of audio-visual aids—non-projected and (if you have the equipment) projected aids—may be demonstrated and discussed.

(5) There may be demonstration and discussion of the use in curriculum enrichment of contemporary materials from books, magazines, newspapers, and life experiences.

Such discussions, exhibits, and demonstrations will open up new vistas of need and opportunity, and disclose a wealth of resources available for the improvement of teaching.

VII. BETTER TEACHING REQUIRES FAVORABLE CONDITIONS

To the *what* and *who* and *why* and *how* must be added the question of *where*—where am I teaching? What conditions are favorable? What conditions are unfavorable?

1. *Investigate Conditions that Affect Teaching*

Many teachers find themselves frustrated by the circumstances which condition their teaching. The difficulties may be physical, emotional, social, intellectual, or spiritual. Sometimes the conditions may be changed through foresight and planning; sometimes they are largely beyond control and must be detoured. In any case, opportunity is afforded in the weekly officers and teachers' meeting to consider favorable and unfavorable conditions of teaching with a view to making maximum use of the favorable and dealing constructively with the unfavorable.

A series of conferences may focus on such factors as:

(1) *Physical conditions.*—Consider how to assure more favorable conditions in respect to: the building, department space, musical instruments and songbooks, classrooms, avoidable and unavoidable distractions, comfort of the pupils, facilities and equipment, lighting and ventilation, and the like.

(2) *Emotional conditions.*—Consider the happy or unhappy relations between pupils and their officers and teachers; the calm or upset feeling of officers, teachers, and pupils as they come together and worship and work together; the eagerness or apathy with which pupils respond.

(3) *Social conditions.*—Examine the agreeableness or tensions which may exist among members of the group due to differences in age or temperament, or to financial, social, or racial distinctions.

(4) *Intellectual conditions.*—Evaluate the ability or inability of officers and teachers to adjust to the mental level of members of the group taught; the variations of levels of intelligence among pupils which create difficulties; the suitability or unsuitability of some of the teaching materials for all members of the department or classes.

(5) *Spiritual conditions.*—Consider the atmosphere of reverence, or its lack, in the department or classes; the attitudes of officers and teachers as they come to their duties; the attitudes of responsiveness or unresponsiveness to spiritual things on the part of pupils; the evidences of concern or unconcern for soul-winning and development in Christian conduct and character; the interest or lack of interest in the worship services; the carry-over of learning into life, or its lack.

2. *Helpful Discussions Should Follow the Investigations*

Discussion periods may be based on such questions as:
What home conditions make teaching more difficult?

What community conditions make teaching more difficult?

What unfavorable conditions in the church building hinder teaching?

How may a more favorable situation for teaching be created by the general or department assembly?

How may the pupils' materials of study be used to better advantage?

How may discomfort, distractions, disturbances be minimized?

How may attention and interest be better maintained?

How may a teacher make sure that the lesson plan will be carried out?

These are matters of basic importance which should be given regular and thoughtful attention. As a result of improved conditions, teaching and the fruits of teaching will be assuredly improved.

VIII. BETTER TEACHING REQUIRES EVALUATION OF RESULTS

What results am I seeking? To the *what* and *who* and *how* and *why* and *where* of teaching must be added *what outcomes*.

1. *Results Should Be Tested*

Officers and teachers may be deceived as to the results of their concern and efforts. The results may be other than those intended or they may be far less than expected. God's Word will not return unto him void, as he has said; but the Word is compared to seed which must have moisture and sunshine, the sower and the harvester, if it is to produce "bread to the eater" (Isa. 55:10–11).

2. *Outcomes of Tests Should Be Discussed*

Opportunity should be provided in the weekly officers and teachers' meeting for discussion and evaluation of results of testing in such areas as:

(1) *Quantitative results.*—Study the growth of the school as a whole; increased enrolment of departments and classes;

new departments and classes formed; attendance goals proposed and reached.

(2) *Qualitative results.*—Make a summary of averages on the Six Point Record System for the school as a whole, an analysis and interpretation of averages by departments and classes, and a checkup on points reached in the Standards and on goals proposed.

(3) *Educative results.*—Consider evidences of interest in Bible study and advances in Bible knowledge; increased responsiveness and participation on the part of the pupils; growth in the effectiveness of teaching; the record of training course awards of officers and teachers; and training goals proposed and reached.

(4) *Evangelistic results.*—Ponder the number won to Christ and baptized into the fellowship of the church, the conversions by departments and classes, evidences of concern and effectiveness in soul-winning by officers and teachers, plans for increased evangelistic efforts, goals proposed.

(5) *Enlistment results.*—Analyze the number of members added to the church by statement or letter, additions by departments and classes, the record of giving, the missionary and service activities, the attendance on preaching and prayer services, the goals proposed.

(6) *Life-changing results.*—Note evidences of transformations in character and conduct through rededications, commitments to full-time Christian service, restorations to fellowship, consecrations to active service, commitments to stewardship-tithing, participation in witnessing and soul-winning.

Seasons of such testing and stock-taking will serve to revitalize the Sunday school and the church as the challenge to advance, based on this evaluation of strong and weak points, is accepted by Sunday school officers and teachers.

IX. Scheduling a Program of Improvement

Obviously not all that needs to be done in the improvement of teaching can be accomplished within the brief limits of the weekly officers and teachers' meeting. This meeting will rather serve as a clearinghouse for determining and scheduling such emphases as those indicated.

1. A Program of Systematic Improvement Is Needed

Two courses will prove fruitful: First, hold occasional meetings of officers and teachers for concentration of attention on one or more of the main matters involved in a consistent program of improvement, devoting either a part or all of the time to this emphasis. Second, set up a series of training courses, or Bible teaching clinics, with meetings at such times as may be suitable. Classes may meet for five consecutive evenings, once or twice a quarter, or for four or five morning or evening meetings (other than on Wednesday night); or departmental meetings may be scheduled according to the convenience of the workers. While such meetings will not be primarily to earn awards, workers should be encouraged to meet all the requirements for credit, as set forth in the back of each training course book.

2. A Schedule by Quarters Is Suggested

The following schedule of emphases by quarters is suggested. Certainly each school and even each department may wish to work out its own schedule, keeping in mind the calendar of activities as adopted for the whole school.

FALL QUARTER: Let Us Improve Ourselves and Our Understanding of Teaching

WINTER QUARTER: Let Us Improve Our Bible Knowledge and Pupil Study

SPRING QUARTER: Let Us Improve Our Aims and Methods

SUMMER QUARTER: Let Us Improve Conditions and Results of Teaching

X. THE CHAPTER SUMMARIZED

1. Better teaching calls for better teachers. The first aim of the teaching improvement period is the enrichment of personality of officers and teachers.

2. Better teaching requires Bible knowledge. A second aim of the teaching improvement period is acquaintance with the Bible as a whole as well as in its several parts.

3. Better teaching requires pupil study. A third aim of the teaching improvement period is understanding those to be taught so that teaching will be person minded.

4. Better teaching requires understanding of teaching. A fourth aim of teaching improvement is mastery of principles as the basis of practice.

5. Better teaching requires clarification of aims. A fifth aim of the teaching improvement period is the making clear and definite of objectives of classroom procedures.

6. Better teaching requires favorable conditions. Good teaching is not dependent on building and equipment but is improved with the provisions of proper facilities.

7. Better teaching requires evaluating results. Teaching will be improved when outcomes are carefully weighed with a view to both qualitative and quantitative increase.

8. Improvement of teaching is made more certain when a schedule for the entire year is planned so as to assure balanced study.

CHAPTER 6

I. THE LESSON MAY BE PRESENTED
   1. The Plan Described
   2. The Plan Evaluated

II. GENERAL PARTICIPATION MAY BE SOUGHT
   1. The Plan Described
   2. The Plan Evaluated

III. THE "ANGLE" METHOD MAY BE USED
   1. The Plan Described
   2. The Plan Evaluated

IV. PREVIOUS ASSIGNMENTS MAY BE FOLLOWED
   1. The Plan Described
   2. The Plan Evaluated

V. A DEMONSTRATION LESSON MAY BE TAUGHT
   1. The Plan Described
   2. The Plan Evaluated

VI. TEACHING PRINCIPLES MAY BE ILLUSTRATED
   1. The Plan Described
   2. The Plan Evaluated

VII. A PLAN SHEET MAY GIVE GUIDANCE
   1. The Plan Described
   2. The Plan Evaluated

VIII. VARIETY IS ESSENTIAL

IX. THE CHAPTER SUMMARIZED

76

6

The Weekly Officers and Teachers'
Meeting Follows a Varied Program

UPON the general superintendent, the general secretary, the minister of education (if any), and the pastor rests chief responsibility for the general period of administration and promotion. Who then is responsible for planning and conducting the periods devoted to department conferences and the improvement of teaching? Obviously, the department superintendents. At no other point in the supervision of the department can the superintendent make a more valuable contribution. Rarely will the meeting rise higher than the level of interest and concern of the department superintendent.

In the class Sunday school, whether workers meet by age groups or the workers in several age groups meet together, one person should be designated in each group to assume the responsibilities which would be ascribed to the department superintendent if there were one.

The department superintendent (or age group leader in the class school) should plan well in advance assignments for the teaching improvement period, endeavoring to give each worker a specific responsibility as often as possible. The superintendent should undertake to provide helpful materials for use in the meetings—visual aids, suggestions from the teacher books and *The Sunday School Builder,* from training course texts, and other books, from magazine articles, and the like.

The superintendent will preside during both the department conference period and the teaching improvement period. He should see to it that each period begins on time, that those who have contributions to make stay within their time limits, and that the meeting closes on time. The superintendent should be a student and an exponent of the art of teaching, and give creative guidance to the practice of this art by those who teach in the department.

Monotony is deadening to attention and interest, yet strangely enough, we are likely to overlook the principle of variety in planning the weekly officers and teachers' meeting. The one best way to conduct the meeting has not yet been found. The worst way, however, is apparent—just repeat the same pattern perennially! There must be change to meet changing needs and interests. What succeeds in one situation may fail in another; what works for awhile may later prove unprofitable. Two questions may be asked that will test any plan: (1) Does it sustain interest? (2) Does it actually improve teaching and learning?

Let us examine some of the principal ways in which the teaching improvement period may be conducted, with evaluation of the strong and weak points of each method.

I. The Lesson May Be Presented

1. *The Plan Described*

The simplest and oldest method of conducting the teaching period is to have someone use the full time to "teach the lesson" very much as it will be taught to a class on Sunday morning. Usually the teacher's chief concern is for exposition, explanation, and illustration of the next lesson, often with emphasis on its application, and sometimes with exhortation to accept and practice the truths brought out.

The procedure may follow the homiletical formula of introduction, two or three points given in exposition, and a conclusion. Again, the teacher may use the method of the examination of context, words and allusions, obvious and implied meanings, direct and indirect teachings, in a verse-by-verse study of the prescribed Bible passage. On occasion, the teacher may lecture on a subject or subjects related to the lesson or series, seeking to provide background for teaching.

2. The Plan Evaluated

One weakness of this method is that too much attention is given to content and too little to method of teaching and adaptation to the needs of various classes. Another weakness is the lack of participation on the part of the group, with consequent ultimate loss of interest.

Then, too, the example of the worker who presents the lesson may induce the teachers who listen to rely too exclusively on the lecture method. Perhaps the gravest objection to this plan for the teaching improvement periods is that it tends to develop mental laziness on the part of teachers, who may come to depend on the one who will present the lesson to do their studying for them. Do we not conclude that this method, while having possible value at times, should be used very sparingly?

II. GENERAL PARTICIPATION MAY BE SOUGHT

1. The Plan Described

The general participation method likewise presupposes a teacher leading in the lesson presentation. In this case the teacher will seek to guide the group in general discussion. He will raise questions to which he will expect answers; and he will give opportunity for questions which he will undertake to answer.

2. The Plan Evaluated

The general participation method is at its best when the teacher uses thought-provoking questions which evoke reflective answers; when the discussion follows an outline that covers the main points of the lesson in hand; and when participation is general and spontaneous, and the discussion is closely related to the Scripture passages. The plan avoids the difficulty of the active teacher and passive listeners. In this, it sets a good example for teachers as they, in turn, seek class participation.

On the other hand, there are obvious weaknesses of this

method. Quite likely there will be concentration on content to the neglect of concern for the interests and needs of those to whom the lesson will be taught. There is always the danger of sidetracking if irrelevant matters are introduced or arguments injected that divert attention from the lesson itself. The time element presents a difficulty, since general participation is time-consuming. Do we not conclude that the disadvantages of this method outweigh the advantages as a routine way of conducting the teaching improvement period?

III. The "Angle" Method May Be Used

1. *The Plan Described*

The "angle" method employs the principle of selectivity. Rather than general participation, responses are sought from selected members of the group under the guidance of the leader of the meeting. Certain "angles" of the lesson are assigned to selected individuals for report, such as:

(1) The context of the lesson, including the "larger lesson" in its general setting and in its connection with the previous lesson

(2) Authorship, time, and place, as those may be significant

(3) Principal characters, if there are biographical references

(4) Important events, if the lesson is narrative

(5) Christian doctrines, if such are directly involved

(6) The central truth or truths

(7) Illustrations

(8) Questions for clarification and discussion

(9) A lesson outline

(10) Conclusion and application

Not all of these "angles" may be presented in any one lesson; usually five or six will suffice and can be given in the allotted time. The leader will tie them together as a "master of ceremonies" and will keep the speakers on schedule.

2. *The Plan Evaluated*

The plan has certain excellences. It provides variety; it utilizes a number of persons; it gives definiteness to participation; it makes possible the sharing of ideas; it concentrates attention on important aspects of the lesson.

Its disadvantages should be noted. It tends to formalize the study, fitting each lesson into a mold. Some of the workers who have been assigned angles may not be present, others may be poorly prepared. The angles may be almost entirely concerned with content and difficult to adapt to specific classes. The presentation of the several angles tends to fragmentation of the lesson so that it is seen as more or less unrelated parts rather than as a whole. Teachers receive very little help as to method of presentation since the angle method would scarcely be practicable in most classes. It is difficult to adapt the plan for workers with young pupils. Experience indicates that this method tends to become tiresome after a time. May we not conclude that the angle method is limited in practicality and value?

IV. PREVIOUS ASSIGNMENTS MAY BE FOLLOWED

1. *The Plan Described*

The "assignment" method seeks to obtain the values and to avoid the weaknesses of the "angle" method. The leader (usually the department superintendent or an assigned officer or teacher) will prepare assignments and suggest resource materials for certain members of the group. The superintendent may get the lesson before the group by reading the Scripture passage or having it read. He himself may present the following points or assign them to someone for presentation:

(1) The central truth of the lesson
(2) The main points of the lesson displayed by means of a chalkboard outline
(3) Problems raised by the lesson as they apply to the pupils in the different classes

With this as background, assigned officers and teachers may, in about five minutes each, present prepared reports:

(1) How to gain attention at the beginning
(2) How to introduce the lesson so as to secure interest and provoke thought
(3) Appropriate ways of presenting the lesson so as to secure class participation
(4) How to relate the lesson to the lives of those taught so as to obtain carry-over into conduct and character

This plan presupposes that the department superintendent will make careful preparation, assist those to whom assignments have been made to find helpful materials, and insist that all officers and teachers bring notebooks and carry away with them the essential ideas presented. The superintendent will, of course, guide the proceedings so that each report is kept in its time limit and all reports are presented.

2. *The Plan Evaluated*

Difficulties of the plan should be taken into account. Some superintendents may not be willing to give the necessary time for preparation; some workers who accept assignments may be careless in preparing and presenting their reports; some may follow the guidance materials literally and unreflectively. May we not conclude that this plan has rich possibilities if superintendents and teachers will take their responsibilities seriously?

V. A DEMONSTRATION LESSON MAY BE TAUGHT

1. *The Plan Described*

By "demonstration lesson" is not meant a lesson taught by an expert to serve as a model. The lesson will be taught by a teacher who takes his or her turn in the weekly meeting. He may tell how he intends to teach the lesson or he may teach a group of the officers and teachers who will represent his Sunday class. In either case, the time will have to be reduced so as to allow ten or fifteen minutes for evaluation. In the

hands of members of the group may be placed mimeographed sheets containing such questions as these:

Did the teacher gain immediate attention? How?
Was interest well sustained?
Was there enough class participation?
Was class participation skilfully guided? How?
Was sufficient emphasis given to the lesson content?
Was the material well adapted to the class?
Was there a spirit of freedom and spontaneity?
Were the questions well phrased and appropriate?
Were the illustrations well chosen?
Was the lesson material effectively outlined?
Did the teacher cover the lesson, avoiding sidetracks?
Did the teacher have an evident aim? What?
Did the aim determine what was included and what was
    omitted from the lesson?
Was the aim measurably achieved?
Was the lesson brought to an effective conclusion?
Was the conclusion applied to lives of the pupils?
Will the lesson probably carry over into life?
What suggestions can be made for improvement?

Not all of these questions can be asked about a given lesson, but some can be selected for each lesson and, over a
period of time, all the questions can be raised.

The questions are never to be asked critically or to the
embarrassment of the teacher. Yet the discussion that follows
the demonstration may bring revolutionary changes, not only
to the demonstrating teacher, but also to all in the group.

2. *The Plan Evaluated*

What are the values of the demonstration lesson? They
are notable: practice under sympathetic observance, correc-
tion of errors that might pass unnoticed in the Sunday class,
the breaking of undesirable habits, the conscious lifting of the
level of skill, the development of confidence before the class
on Sunday after the Wednesday experience, sharing that
enriches the entire group.

What are the difficulties? Some teachers are reluctant to teach a demonstration lesson, others refuse outright; teaching conditions are abnormal and may put the teacher at a disadvantage; time is more limited than on Sunday, hence the lesson must be abbreviated; comments may lack relevance and insight; the procedure may become superficial. The plan is difficult to adapt for workers with Nursery, Beginner, and Primary groups. Are we not warranted, however, in the judgment that the plan has great value when properly carried out and that it should be used frequently?

VI. TEACHING PRINCIPLES MAY BE ILLUSTRATED

An advanced step is made when teachers are led to consider and apply basic principles of teaching to the preparation and presentation of lessons. They thus become increasingly independent of "helps," whether personal or printed. They learn to develop their own lesson plans and originate their own methods of teaching.

Teachers may justifiably complain that following the ideas and outlines of others fails to give them the confidence they need through mastery of underlying principles, and that study of principles of teaching in a textbook often fails to carry over into actual teaching procedures. These difficulties may be met by the effective relating of principles and practice.

1. *The Plan Described*

Preceding the study of a given lesson or series, the superintendent may concentrate attention on certain principles of teaching set forth in a training course book or books. Officers and teachers should supply themselves with the text or texts and study them at home by the individual plan. In the meetings the chapters may or may not be used seriatim, but spotlighted at the point where a principle is involved that is related to the lesson or lessons to be taught.

For instance, the principle may be that of "learning by wholes rather than by parts." The principle having been stated and made understandable, there then may be a presentation of "preview studies," according to which the entire series or unit will be seen as a whole.

The principle may be that of "learning through responding." Reports may be presented by the workers, with a view to gaining maximum class response through the use of Bibles, questions, and guided discussion.

The principle may be that of "gaining attention and holding interest." Search of a given lesson may be made to discover at each main point that which will command attention which can then be deepened into interest.

The principle may be that of "stimulating and organizing thought through questions." Applied to next Sunday's lesson, various types of questions may be proposed and discussed, with a view to perfecting the art of questioning.

The principle may be "from the known to the unknown," with concentration on the problem of finding and using illustrations from that which is familiar to clarify and illuminate that which is unfamiliar.

The principle may be that of "creative thinking through discussion." The lesson may be dealt with as a problem whose solution is to be found through the sharing of differences and agreements, until, in the light of the teaching of the lesson, consensus is reached.

The principle may be that of "teaching to effect changes." The several parts of the lesson may then be presented with the question uppermost: What changes in understanding, in attitudes, in choices, in conduct, and in character are we seeking in this lesson or series?

2. *The Plan Evaluated*

The advantages of this plan are many. It combines the study of lessons with the study of textbooks on teaching; it relates theory to practice; it gives opportunity to test the principles in actual situations; it encourages independent and creative thinking; it gives teachers a sense of mastery in that their methods have the support of fundamental truths; it provides for growth, both in personality and proficiency, and thus saves from shallowness and superficiality.

That there are difficulties is evident—the unwillingness of some officers and teachers to give the necessary time to the study of the textbooks, the problem of relating the appropriate principle to a given lesson, the danger of becoming too academic and thus losing some of the force of the Scripture passages studied, lack of time for thoroughness in discussion and application of the principle involved. May we not conclude, however, that this plan has great potentiality and deserves recurrent use?

VII. A Plan Sheet May Give Guidance

Distinction should be made between a "lesson outline" and a "teaching plan." The lesson outline undertakes to state in a phrase or sentence each of the main points of the Scripture passage or passages around which the lesson exposition will be gathered. The teaching plan proposes a step-by-step procedure in getting into the experience of the learners, through the personality of the teacher, those truths of the lesson which have been selected to meet the specific needs of the persons to be taught. The function of the teaching improvement period of the officers and teachers' meeting will therefore be chiefly to stimulate and guide in the development of appropriate teaching plans.

1. *The Plan Described*

Before the actual lesson plan is considered, the superintendent may present a brief recall of the unit, the unit aim, and the relation which the lesson bears to the unit. The notes made during the preview study should refresh each worker's memory on these points.

The superintendent may then lead the group to consider the specific needs of the individual pupils which this lesson should meet. Let them read the basic Scripture passages, recall the lesson title, and state the main guiding truths involved.

A practical "plan sheet" will guide the workers as together they prepare a teaching guide for use on Sunday. For the younger groups, where teaching is planned around centers of activity, the plan sheet will follow the pattern set forth in the free literature and the training course book on teaching for the age group involved.

For older groups, the plan sheet would provide for consideration of:

Lesson aim
Central truth, or central problem
Plan for securing interest
Procedure to stimulate and guide pupil participation
Difficulties to avoid
Ways of leading pupils to relate the lesson to their own lives
Suggestions for stimulating interest in the next lesson

The activity program for the younger age groups requires a different type of plan sheet. The procedure will be planned, not by "lessons" but by guided experiences to be provided through various activities. The plan sheet would include such items as the following:

Teaching purpose
Name of the activity
Materials needed
Bible stories
Pictures
Bible verses
Songs
Anticipated prayer opportunities
Desired results

Plans for Primary, Beginner, and older Nursery departments would include procedures for activity time and for group time. Suggested forms for plan sheets will be found in the free literature and the training course books on teaching for the various age groups.

2. *The Plan Evaluated*

Such a "plan sheet" obviously calls for more than can be covered in a given teaching improvement period, hence the necessity of having workers come with the steps in the plan tentatively noted, and the need for selection on the part of the leader regarding the steps to receive major attention during the teaching improvement period.

Values of the plan are readily noted—guidance of systematic preparation, focusing of attention on both content and class, development of the lesson both logically and psychologically, step-by-step progress toward a satisfying conclusion, a plan of preparation that at the same time provides a plan of presentation.

Difficulties inhere in the comprehensiveness of the plan—time requirements are heavy, teachers may lack resources for the study, inexperienced teachers may find themselves out of their depth. Notwithstanding the difficulties, does not this plan commend itself as giving promise of rich returns on the investment of time and thought?

VIII. VARIETY IS ESSENTIAL

Here have been set forth seven plans which afford wide variety for the conduct of the weekly officers and teachers' meeting. A method suitable for one situation might be unsuitable for another. What works well in one department might fail in another. High interest and attendance might be maintained one quarter, but decline the next under the same plan. We therefore conclude that a successful officers and teachers' meeting, to be sustained year in and year out, calls for a variety of plans, all of which must be submitted to the twofold test of sustained interest on the part of officers and teachers and practical value in the improvement of teaching.

IX. THE CHAPTER SUMMARIZED

1. An exposition of the lesson may be made by someone well versed in the Scriptures. This method, failing to secure participation, will seldom prove satisfactory.

2. The leader may seek general participation through questions and answers. This method, emphasizing and clarifying content, may not afford enough help for the improvement of teaching procedures.

3. The lesson may be studied from a number of "angles" presented by selected officers and teachers. This method, while providing variety and participation, may give insufficient attention to methods of teaching.

4. Previous assignments may be made calling for reports by designated officers and teachers. This plan has the advantage of including emphasis on both content and method.

5. The lesson may be taught by a selected officer or teacher, with opportunity for critical evaluation by the other officers and teachers. This plan provides practice both in teaching and in judging the effectiveness of teaching.

6. The lesson may be so presented as to illustrate a principle of teaching. This plan effectually brings together theory and practice.

7. The co-operative study of the lesson may follow a "plan sheet." The definite procedures give guidance to teachers both in preparing and in presenting the lesson.

8. No one of the plans proposed should be used continuously. Sustained interest and cumulative values call for variety.

CHAPTER 7

I. CONSIDER THE FELLOWSHIP MEAL
   1. The Meal Is Desirable
   2. The Meal Is Not Indispensable

II. SCHEDULE THE PROMOTIONAL PERIODS
   1. Follow a Definite Schedule for the General Period
   2. Attend to Promotional Matters for the Department
   3. Adjust the Schedule in the School Organized on the Class Basis

III. MAINTAIN EFFICIENT ORGANIZATION
   1. Points for Emphasis Noted
   2. Timely Items Selected

IV. PROMOTE ATTENDANCE AND GROWTH
   1. Results from Records Utilized
   2. Visitation of Absentees Promoted
   3. Search for New Members Systematized

V. SEEK TEACHING IMPROVEMENT
   1. Cradle Roll Improvement Period
   2. Nursery Improvement Period
   3. Beginner Improvement Period
   4. Primary Improvement Period
   5. Junior Improvement Period

VI. THE CHAPTER SUMMARIZED

7

The Weekly Officers and Teachers' Meeting in Action

"Show us how it works!" From the curious child to the inquiring adult, this demand arises when something new or different is offered. The description may be attractive and the promise enticing, but the question persists, How does it work? An undertaking may begin with a flourish, but we want to know, Will it hold out? The proposal may be inviting, but we want to know, Is it worth what it costs?

Many Sunday schools have answered these questions affirmatively through successful experience over many years with the weekly officers and teachers' meeting. Other schools have found difficulties in maintaining the meeting and are seeking courageously to overcome them. Still others, convinced of the need and the value of the meeting, would be helped to inaugurate it if they had something in the nature of a blueprint which gave details as to its operation. This chapter and the next, which are based on the study of several hundred typical situations, propose to picture the officers and teachers' meeting in action in a variety of situations.

I. Consider the Fellowship Meal

Some of the most successful officers and teachers' meetings are preceded by a fellowship meal. This serves a number of purposes.

1. *The Meal Is Desirable*

The meal enables people who are employed to come immediately from their work to the church.

The meal makes possible the Wednesday service as a family affair. Parents, children, and even guests can gather around the table and as of old "eat their meat with gladness and singleness of heart" (Acts 2:46).

The plan provides opportunity for dissemination of information during the meal. It facilitates acquaintanceship and fellowship; members come to know one another better and to love one another more.

In the larger church a hostess is usually employed to buy the food and supervise its preparation. In the smaller situation, departments or classes may take turns in providing and preparing the meal. If kitchen facilities are lacking, a "pot luck" meal may be served, designated families taking their turn in bringing items of food which, when combined, make a satisfactory meal.

Almost invariably there is a nominal charge for the meal unless the food is furnished by families. In most cases an amount is put in the budget to keep the cost down and yet insure that the meal will be satisfying. Departments or classes rotate in serving the meal and clearing the tables. The values of the meal are so evident and real that churches are more and more adopting the plan.

2. *The Meal Is Not Indispensable*

To the question, "Is the meal indispensable?" the answer is, "No, but a great convenience." There are situations in which the serving of the meal would be admittedly difficult. In some communities the church members are scattered, they live at a distance from the church, their work hours interfere. In many churches there are no facilities for serving the meal. Let it not be concluded that these obstacles seriously interfere with the weekly officers and teachers' meeting. The time may be moved up thirty to forty-five minutes if necessary. Sometimes light refreshments may be served as the people arrive—coffee or tea and cookies—to add a touch of social fellowship.

Promptly at the time set, say 6:45 or 7:00 o'clock, the meeting will begin with song and prayer. Then, for fifteen minutes, general administrative and promotional matters will be given attention just as would be the case if there had been a preceding meal. After the general promotional period, there will be, if possible, an hour for conferences in the departments or age groups. This one-hour period will include the department promotional conferences and the teaching improvement session, just as in a school where the meal is served. The essential matter is not the meal, but a well-prepared and attractive program dealing with those things that concern all officers and teachers.

II. SCHEDULE THE PROMOTIONAL PERIODS

In the promotional periods led by the general superintendent and the department superintendents the schedule will include some, or all, of the items indicated:

1. *Follow a Definite Schedule for the General Period*

PRAYER

ROLL CALL BY DEPARTMENTS: Note number of workers present and number absent.

STUDY OF RECORDS: Show last Sunday's highlights indicated on the Six Point Record System; compare with last Sunday, last year, or accepted goal; diagnose main weakness revealed and indicate remedial work.

SPECIAL EMPHASIS: Base on calendar of activities and plans made in the superintendent's cabinet or workers' council.

OBJECTIVES AND RECOGNITIONS: Present, promote, and check on current goals; recognize special achievements (such as 100 per cent classes, departments with all workers present, training awards earned, goals reached, Standards attained); recognize visitors; welcome new church members.

ADJOURNMENT WITH PRAYER: Officers and teachers go immediately to department conferences.

2. *Attend to Promotional Matters for the Department*

Following the general period, workers should meet by departments (or by age groups in the class Sunday school).

Under the direction of the department superintendent, matters of promotion will be given attention. The department promotion will correlate with the promotion in the general period, and will usually include such items as:

(1) Roll call of teachers and officers
(2) Supply arranged for any teacher or officer who anticipates absence next Sunday
(3) Distribution of names of absentees and prospects to be visited, visitation reports received
(4) Noting last Sunday's records with emphasis on high and low points
(5) Periodic checking of the department Standard, recognition of Standard classes
(6) Brief stress on any special event project, or problem needing current attention
(7) Explanation of special features of the assembly program or activities for the large group
(8) Prayer for special objects and for divine guidance of next Sunday's session

Of course not all of these objects will ordinarily be on the agenda each time. Assuming one hour for the department period, about fifteen minutes must suffice for this aspect of the meeting.

Superintendents of departments justify their titles and discharge their duties more adequately by their planning and conduct of the department periods of the weekly officers and teachers' meeting than by any other function. Cradle Roll and Extension superintendents will find in the literature for their departments suggested patterns for their weekly workers' meetings.

3. *Adjust the Schedule in the School Organized on the Class Basis*

If the Sunday school is organized on the class basis, most of the promotional matters will be cared for in the general period. Then the workers may meet according to the Standard age groups to take care of any of the matters pertaining to the age group which may not have been sufficiently cared for in the general period. In each group an individual should be designated as leader, to function as a department superintendent would, if there were such an officer in the group. In very small schools, it may be expedient to group Nursery and Beginner workers; Primary and Junior teachers; Intermediate, Young People, and Adult teachers. Such combinations should be avoided if possible. In even the smallest school there should be a Cradle Roll department and an Extension department, each maintaining its own weekly workers' meeting.

III. MAINTAIN EFFICIENT ORGANIZATION

A clock not wound up runs down. Machinery not kept in repair gets out of order. The human body not cared for is subject to illness. The Sunday school organization is like the clock, the machine, the human body. Requirements of effective administration must be met or the school runs down, the machinery creaks, the organism suffers. During the general and department promotional periods, as indicated in the schedule, the following matters should be considered.

1. *Points for Emphasis Should Be Noted*

What must we do week by week in the general or department promotional periods to keep the organization at peak efficiency? These are answers that come from Sunday schools whose officers and teachers meet every week:

Check the roll to discover if any officer or teacher expects to be absent on Sunday, and plan to supply a teacher for the class temporarily or permanently if necessary.

Call attention to last Sunday's records, indicating high and low averages on the Six Point System and giving recognitions where such are due.

Compare the records with those for last Sunday and last year and stress enrolment and attendance goals.

Consider any matters of scheduling that need attention—starting and dismissing on time, preventing interferences and distractions, and other adjustments that may be needed.

Make announcements concerning special emphases and events and lead workers to catch step in carrying out common purposes.

Carry out recommendations from the superintendent's cabinet, according to plans made in the monthly council.

Recognize new officers and teachers and introduce visitors.

2. Timely Items Selected

Of course not all of these things will be done at every meeting. From the list, selection will be made in accordance with timeliness and need. Every item should be carefully considered in advance and its presentation so timed as to keep within the limit of fifteen minutes. It should be borne in mind that the promotional periods are not business meetings of the church nor are they "debating societies." The purpose of the general and department promotional periods is to keep the organization functioning at top efficiency.

IV. PROMOTE ATTENDANCE AND GROWTH

Some institutions may compel attendance by law or by threat of penalty. Sunday school attendance is purely voluntary. Those who attend must feel profited and those who are absent must feel that they are missed.

1. Results from Records Utilized

It is of utmost importance that accurate records be kept so that officers and teachers will know exactly who are present and who are absent each Sunday and the extent to which each pupil has co-operated and developed in such basic matters as punctuality, Bible brought, offering made, lesson studied, preaching service attended.

"Out of sight is out of mind." We must therefore bring to the attention of officers and teachers, week by week, an analysis of the records: (1) number enrolled, (2) number present, (3) number absent, (4) number on time, (5) number with Bibles, (6) number with offering, (7) number studied lessons, (8) number attending worship service, (9) significance of totals by departments and classes.

These points vary with the several age groups. Nursery children are graded only on one point—present. Beginners and Primaries are graded on two points—present and on time. Extension department members grade themselves on lessons studied, daily Bible readings and offering.

To read lists of figures is tedious and time-consuming. A better way is to have them posted on a chalkboard, with appropriate columns permanently ruled and lettered, or to have the reports mimeographed and distributed to the people at the beginning of the general period. A few moments will be given to analyzing and interpreting the totals.

2. *Visitation of Absentees Promoted*

On the basis of the records exhibited, plans can be made to maintain a higher average of attendance. It is alarming when attendance is 50 per cent, or less, of enrolment. It is a matter of grave concern when it is between 50 and 60 per cent. The aim for the entire school should be not less than 75 per cent, not counting the Cradle Roll or Extension departments.

To maintain such an average attendance requires every-week attention in the general and department periods. The associate superintendent (general or department) whose responsibility is attendance should lead in doing the following things: (1) Note each absentee; see that each teacher has a record of his absentees. (2) Plan a program of personal contacts through cards, telephone calls, personal visits. This will be carried out through teachers and, in the case of older pupils, through the class officers. (3) Plan prayerful investigation if the absence is extended over a period of three or four weeks. (4) Drop a name only after authorization by the general superintendent and department superintendent.

If these activities are carried out faithfully and regularly, absenteeism can be greatly reduced.

3. *Search for New Members Systematized*

Seeking prospective members must be continuous. The associate superintendent whose special responsibility is attendance and enlargement should be given two or three minutes in which to implement this work also. He will: (1) Secure and analyze the reports of the total number of visits and other contacts made to prospects each week. (2) Receive information on new prospects discovered. (3) See that prospects are correctly assigned (to departments or teachers, as the case may be). (4) Promote the visitation plan adopted by the Sunday school in line with the policy of the church.

Any Sunday school can be made to grow if, week by week, attention is concentrated on specific persons to be sought by specific persons for enrolment in units with clearly defined constituency. The most effective channel for continuous promotion of a sustained program of visitation is the regular weekly officers and teachers' meeting.

V. SEEK TEACHING IMPROVEMENT

The period devoted to the improvement of teaching should be, not "thirty golden minutes," but forty-five. Since it is for fruitful teaching that the Sunday school exists, the time devoted to preparation for better teaching is the most precious time of the weekly meeting. Every precaution should be taken to protect this period.

Full provision should be made for every department, including the Cradle Roll and Extension.

In the larger schools with multiple departments, the teachers and officers of each department will usually meet separately, although on rare occasions there may be combined meetings of all the workers within an age group. Superintendents may take the items indicated in the suggestions which follow and select those that are relevant for a given meeting. They may be reproduced on a "plan sheet" for distribution to teachers and specific assignments indicated. With plans thus made in advance, there should never be a dull session. Certainly all planning must be carried out in complete dependence upon the Holy Spirit for guidance and empowering. His ministry is teaching (John 14:26). He fully knows all pupil needs and how to meet them.

1. Cradle Roll Improvement Period

The Cradle Roll department ministers to homes where there are children from birth through three years of age. Its aim is "A Christian home for every baby." It is as definite a part of the Sunday school as any other department. Its superintendent and visitors should be in the weekly officers and teachers' meeting and should devote their department session to planning and to intensification of concern for their teaching ministries. Their discussions will gather around such educational emphases as the following:

(1) Consider parent education, with a view to visits in the home that will enrich the understanding of the parents concerning their privileges and responsibilities as teachers of the child.

(2) Briefly review books dealing with child care and nurture which may be safely recommended to parents.

(3) Discuss problems which have been confronted in certain homes and how these problems may be dealt with in the interest of the Cradle Roll child.

(4) Make plans for parent-worker meetings and for individual conferences with parents, designed for mutual helpfulness.

(5) Call attention to such materials as free literature on Cradle Roll work, *Messages to Cradle Roll Parents,* appropriate articles in *The Sunday School Builder, Home Life, Living with Children,* and other sources.

(6) Discuss ways in which Cradle Roll workers can cooperate with Nursery workers in the interest of children and parents.

(7) Pray for unsaved and unchurched parents, and share experiences as to how they can be won to Christ and to church membership.

(8) Discuss ways to assist parents to establish a plan for family worship, using suggestions from *Home Life* magazine.

(9) Plan for weekday activities—reports of visits made,

assignment of visits to be made, new babies enrolled, Cradle Roll children transferred to Nursery, helps suggested to meet parents' needs, special prayer for the children and their parents, etc.

2. Nursery Improvement Period

Nursery workers need to realize that they are among the most important teachers in the Sunday school. Theirs is far more than a "baby-sitting" responsibility. By loving care and cheerful spirit they teach the babies that God is love and that the church is a place of happiness and security. They teach the two- and three-year-olds more directly by actions and words, and so build foundations for the child's understanding and appreciation of the Bible, the church, and the love of God revealed in Christ. Like that of the Cradle Roll workers, theirs is also a ministry to the home. Thus they will be deeply concerned for such matters as the home life of each child, the help they can give to parents that each child may have a Christian home, and planned visits in the home to secure co-operation in achieving the aims of the Nursery department. The teaching improvement period of the department will include such matters as:

(1) Attend to physical aspects, such as clean linens for the baby beds, sterilized bottles containing each baby's formula, if needed, fruit juices and crackers as desired, comfortable lighting and temperature control, orderly arrangement of chairs, playthings, and the like.

(2) Look at the superintendent's record book and the group record books; add items to the cumulative record in each worker's loose-leaf book concerning changing needs and interests of each child.

(3) Share experiences with a view to correcting any difficulties that may have arisen the previous Sunday.

(4) Consider ways by which each child may be made to feel that Sunday school is a friendly, happy place where he may have pleasant experiences which assure him that he is accepted and loved.

(5) For the two- and three-year-olds, carefully arrange

the materials needed for each activity and plan for co-operative guidance of the children as they take part in the various activities. (See plan sheet.)

(6) Study the printed helps, lift out and discuss those suggestions which apply especially to the local situation.

(7) Give especial consideration to "problem children." Perhaps suggest that the parent of a difficult child bring him or her to the department during the week. Plan discussion with "difficult parents" whose personal attitudes may contribute to the problem.

(8) Occasionally, show pictures or review books that give insight into child life.

(9) Make provision for the extended session during the preaching service.

(10) Complete the preparation for Sunday—rooms and equipment made ready; needed materials available and in place; reception of children planned; purposes for Sunday sessions proposed; plans shared for use of stories, pictures, Bible verses, songs and prayers; experiences of last Sunday shared; special problems discussed; co-operation of parents sought through visits to homes; extended session provided for.

3. *Beginner Improvement Period*

Children four and five present one of the most demanding and rewarding opportunities of the Sunday school for effective teaching. These children are active, inquiring, imitative, imaginative, impressionable. What is done for them during these years may determine destiny. Perhaps no group needs to come together for conferences more than workers with Beginners. These children are not to be thought of as "classes" to be exposed to "lessons," but as distinctive persons in group situations who are learning from every element that enters into their experience, from the time they reach the church building until they leave. As the workers with Beginners come together for the teaching improvement period they will include in their consideration such activities as:

(1) Review last Sunday's experiences with a view to

strengthening weak points. Discuss behavior problems which may have developed.

(2) Share experiences from observation of the children or from visits to their homes.

(3) Plan for using the teaching opportunities which occur as the children engage in various activities.

(4) Suggest ways in which each child's experience may be happy and character-building.

(5) Concentrate attention on the lesson materials, following a lesson plan form which will include: the unit topic, the lesson purpose, the Bible story to be introduced, the recall stories to be used, the Bible verse for the day, and the pupil activities such as singing, praying, relaxing, and using Bible verses.

(6) Consider the plans presented by the superintendent for the group period.

(7) Share the cumulative information for the notebook "life history" of each child.

(8) Occasionally use a motion picture or filmstrip which will give insight into child life, or review enriching books on the subject.

(9) Pray for greater capacity to love and appreciate each child.

4. *Primary Improvement Period*

Primary children, six to eight, have reached the "individualizing stage." Each child needs personal study, personal attention, personal care. Superintendents must provide programs that make room for initiative and participation; teachers must personalize their teaching. Lessons unrelated to life, regimented activities, and rote memory drill may dry up interest in the Bible and develop dislike for Sunday school.

Officers and teachers should realize that they can scarcely hope to fulfil their duty toward these children unless they meet regularly for prayer and planning. Since the youngest Primaries are approaching reading age and the oldest are well advanced in school, officers and teachers should seek to make every moment of the child's time in Sunday school rich in content and satisfaction. In the teaching improvement period workers should concentrate their attention especially on such activities as the following. The plan sheet in the *Primary Superintendent's Manual, Book One* offers helpful guidance.

(1) Make a quick evaluation of last Sunday's session.

(2) Briefly preview the new unit (when a new unit is reached).

(3) Consider pupil needs to be met through next Sunday's program (activity time and group time).

(4) Consider the teaching aim in the light of pupil needs, proposed activities, materials in the pupil book, and suggestions in the teacher book.

(5) Consider interests and experiences of pupils which relate to the unit with a view to using these experiences as the basis for teaching.

(6) Suggest ways to use the Bible in proposed activities. Choose ways to use the Bible verse and to make it meaningful.

(7) Suggest ways to guide pupil participation in conversation in group time.

(8) Choose pictures that are closely related to the Bible truth of the unit and discuss ways to use them in group time.

(9) Talk about ways to help the child use his book satisfactorily at home and to help him have weekday experiences with the truth that he learned about on Sunday.

(10) Share ideas as to other appropriate materials, such as nature objects, clippings from magazines, illustrative missionary objects. Share incidents, ideas, and other materials that will enrich teaching on Sunday morning.

(11) Make co-operative preparation for other phases of the Sunday morning procedure.

(12) Talk about opportunities for worship which the planned experiences are expected to provide.

(13) Recognize dependence upon God for his leadership. Every step of the planning should be done prayerfully.

Such group study will bring many enriching ideas to the workers as they plan together for Sunday morning.

5. *Junior Improvement Period*

Juniors are becoming more group-minded and are developing increasing capacity for teamwork. They are growing in the ability to judge for themselves, to appraise situations and evaluate conduct—their own and others'. These are the years when it is natural for boys and girls to make a decision for Christ, to trust Jesus as Saviour and to follow him as Leader. The Junior who leaves the department without having become a Christian is in danger of missing the way forever.

Those who work with Juniors in the Sunday school dare not take their responsibility lightly. Needs of these group-minded boys and girls must be met with co-operative preparation on the part of officers and teachers. They can scarcely hope to achieve best results unless they come together week by week to share in planning. In using certain of the procedures suggested in chapter 6, Junior superintendents may make such adaptations as the following:

(1) If there are only two classes (one for boys and one for girls) for each of the four grades, those who teach nines and tens may meet together, those who teach elevens and twelves may meet together. Attention may be concentrated on each lesson alternately, teachers sharing with one another as to how the lesson may be taught most effectively.

(2) Occasionally, the lesson may be taught as if to a given class of Juniors, with discussion and evaluation by the other teachers.

(3) Better still, aspects of the teaching procedure may be discussed, such as: how to make an interesting beginning; what questions to ask; apt illustrations to be used; explanations of difficulties to be made; purposeful use of the Bible; attractive use of pictures, maps, objects, and other helps; how to stimulate and guide participation on the part of pupils, especially in the use of the Bible; how to utilize unexpected teaching opportunities; how to encourage memory work by making it meaningful; how to utilize the active

energies of pupils; how to relate the lesson to the pupils' lives so that it will carry over into conduct and character.

(4) The department assembly program (which should follow the class period) should be considered as a means of deepening the impressions made during the lesson period.

(5) Specific lesson preparation may be varied by relating it to the principles set forth in the book *Better Bible Teaching for Juniors,* and showing how these principles can be applied.

For variety, the superintendent may plan a discussion of "Problems in Teaching Juniors": getting attention, holding interest, using Bibles, securing memory work and homework, dealing with inattentiveness and disorder, asking and answering questions, guiding pupil participation, using the lesson materials, introducing pictures and extra-lesson materials, knowing the pupil's home life and school life, discovering pupil's interests, leading pupils to Christ and to church membership, and other matters related to the local situation.

VII. THE CHAPTER SUMMARIZED

1. The fellowship meal, while not indispensable, can be provided in a variety of ways and should be given consideration as a factor in the success of the weekly meeting.

2. A definite schedule should be devised for the promotional periods of the meeting and, with necessary variations, followed faithfully and regularly. Following the general promotional period, meetings by departments or by age groups should give brief attention to promotional matters.

3. The maintenance of efficient organization requires that in both the general and the department promotional periods attention be given regularly to significant and timely details.

4. Higher levels of attendance and increased enrolment result from planning based on accurate records and known possibilities rather than on wishful thinking.

5. The most important aspect of the officers and teachers' meeting is the period devoted to improvement of teaching, presided over by the respective department superintendents, with attention concentrated on preparation for next Sunday.

CHAPTER 8

I. SEEK IMPROVEMENT IN THE OLDER DEPARTMENTS
   1. A Pattern May Be Followed
   2. Teaching Improvement Periods for Intermediate Workers
   3. Teaching Improvement Periods for Young People's Workers
   4. Teaching Improvement Periods for Adult Workers
   5. Teaching Improvement Periods for Extension Workers

II. SEEK TEACHING IMPROVEMENT IN CLASS SCHOOLS
   1. Department Procedures Must Be Adapted
   2. Limitations Heighten Obligation

III. SHARE THE HOUR OF PRAYER
   1. The Prayer Meeting Must Be Preserved
   2. The Prayer Meeting Can Be Vitalized

IV. THE CHAPTER SUMMARIZED

106

8

The Weekly Officers and Teachers'
Meeting in Action

[*Continued*]

WORKERS WITH CHILDREN, as we have seen, have much in common. Officers and teachers who deal with the age groups from Nursery through Junior constitute a natural division of the Sunday school. In a special way they should understand one another's plans and purposes, problems and difficulties. They would do well occasionally to have a joint meeting in which they would share their common interests and aims. Such a meeting should not be held at the weekly officers and teachers' meeting hour.

I. SEEK IMPROVEMENT IN THE OLDER DEPARTMENTS

Workers with Intermediates, Young People, and Adults likewise have much in common. Intermediates are moving rapidly toward becoming Young People and Young People will soon be Adults. These workers also constitute a natural division of the Sunday school, and they likewise would do well to keep themselves informed about one another's plans. For them also an occasional joint conference will be helpful. For both groups, the elementary workers and the workers with the older classes and departments, the joint conference should be on some other evening than Wednesday and include social features which will develop acquaintance and deepen fellowship. Since the ministry of Extension department workers is mainly to the older groups, they may be included in such a conference.

We turn now to the weekly officers and teachers' meeting in action as we view the older sections.

1. *A Pattern May Be Followed*

The various procedures discussed in chapter 6 lend themselves most effectively to use with workers in departments above the Junior age.

In any of the groups of workers in the older departments certain items will be considered from time to time. The activities listed are adaptable for teaching improvement periods for workers with Intermediates, Young People, or Adults.

(1) Recall last Sunday's teaching procedure with a view to evaluation and improvement.

(2) Consider the unit of lessons and its relevance to characteristic needs of the various ages included in the department.

(3) Determine the central truth, or the main truths, in the lesson for the next Sunday. This may involve reports dealing with the content of the lesson.

(4) Exchange ideas and use helps to clarify any difficulties in the Scripture passages on which the lesson is based.

(5) Consider the interests which are absorbing individual class members during the week; seek to understand the moral and spiritual problems they are confronting; and determine what there is in the unit and in the particular lesson under consideration which relates to each member's current needs.

(6) State the lesson aim in terms of pupil interests and needs.

(7) Determine some approaches to the lesson to make it "come alive" for specific classes.

(8) Prepare ways to stimulate and guide thinking, Bible searching and discussion in order to lead pupils to experience truths which relate to the lesson aim.

(9) Consider ways to lead pupils to relate the lesson to their own lives, and to secure carry-over into weekday living.

(10) Share experiences, ideas, resources, and prayer to the end that teachers and officers may themselves be enriched.

From the foregoing list of activities a "plan sheet" may be prepared for distribution to the officers and teachers, who may use it for guidance in preparing for the discussion in the teaching improvement periods. In the light of the group discussion, each teacher should seek to revise and improve his proposed teaching procedure.

2. Teaching Improvement Periods for Intermediate Workers

Boys and girls thirteen to sixteen are no longer "children." They have reached the time when adjustments are being made in all areas of their lives—physically, mentally, socially, spiritually. If they have been in Sunday school through the Junior years, they can be presumed to have a fair background of Bible knowledge. Many will have accepted Christ and become church members. Those who are unsaved should be the object of prayer and concern until they too have made the decision.

Officers and teachers of Intermediates must realize that they are dealing with life at one of its most difficult stages. Careless and superficial preparation is inexcusable and the best preparation cannot be made without co-operative study and planning. Far more is involved than the presentation of the lesson on Sunday morning, no matter how effectively that may be done. Every teacher and officer should therefore be present every Wednesday evening to consider such matters as those listed in the foregoing pattern.

For variety, there may be a series of discussions of "Intermediates and How to Teach Them." For background material have workers use the Intermediate training course book on teaching (for individual home study). In the discussion in the weekly meeting, relate the study of the book to the current lesson series.

For a specified period the weekly meetings may feature discussions on "Understanding Intermediates." Workers may use an appropriate textbook for background study, and relate it to their firsthand observations of individual pupils, made through acquaintance with them at church, in their homes, in their school life, in their play and social activities, and in their work life.

At another time there may be a series of discussions on "Winning Intermediates to Christ," which will involve using an appropriate textbook for source material and outside study; noting opportunities for soul-winning in the current lessons; planning personal conversations with unsaved pupils; enlisting the help of the pastor; and joining in concerted prayer for unsaved Intermediates, whether in the Sunday school or unenrolled.

3. *Teaching Improvement Periods for Young People's Workers*

Appeals for time and energy multiply as young people reach the seventeen- through twenty-four age. It is the period of adventure, of romance, of aspiration and temptation, of success and failure. Officers and teachers who work with these young people need one another's help. As they come together for the teaching improvement period, they will concentrate attention on teaching for results.

Variation may be provided through home study of an appropriate training course book on teaching, with the application each week of a principle of teaching to the lesson to be taught.

Again, there may be a series of discussions on "Meeting the Needs of Young People with the Bible." Consideration should be given to such interests and needs as: education, vocation, social life, recreation, amusement, ambition, temptation, intellectual doubt, moral confusion, courtship and marriage. Current lessons should be related to these problems as giving guidance to their solution.

At another time there may be a discussion of "How to Teach Young People," using selected teachers who will discuss such methods as the lecture, the discussion, the use of stories and illustrations, asking and answering questions, dramatization, role-playing, instituting and conducting projects. One or more weekly meetings may be given to discussions of "Winning Young People to Christ and Enlisting Them for Service." These discussions may be based on an appropriate soul-winning text (which workers may study by the individual method). The discussions should be accompanied by actual experience in dealing with unsaved young people in and out of Sunday school. Another series of discussions may use the theme "Understanding Young People," based on an appropriate text as background material. Workers in the Young People Away department will adjust their meetings according to the needs of their work. (See leaflets on the work of this department.)

4. *Teaching Improvement Periods for Adult Workers*

Most adults are chiefly interested in the "teachings" of the lesson. As a rule, they are hungry for Bible knowledge but often are accustomed to listening to the results of the teacher's Bible study. Teachers should realize that the full needs of adults are not met by a lecture on the lesson. Through co-operative study, lesson procedures can be discovered which make unnecessary the reliance on the lecture as the sole method of teaching.

Variety may be secured by occasional use of other plans, such as are suggested in chapter 6. There may be a series of discussions of "Adults and Their Difficulties," considering such matters as home life, work life, parent-child relationships, Christian neighborliness, Christian citizenship, Christian social life, temptations of adulthood, preventing spiritual decline, dealing with moral problems, maintaining intellectual alertness, practicing missions and soul-winning, being good stewards, the Christian in business.

At another time there may be a series of discussions on "Winning and Enlisting Adults" based on the home study of appropriate textbooks and accompanied by practice in the art of visiting, personal witnessing, enlisting others in service. All these activities should be related to the lessons being studied.

5. *Teaching Improvement Periods for Extension Workers*

Extension workers need to be in the weekly officers and teachers' meetings as much as any others. Theirs too is a teaching ministry. The following schedule may be used for the four or five weekly meetings each month. These suggestions may be adapted to fit the needs of the workers. Although not all of the topics can be used at one time, during the course of the year most of these listed, and others also, will need to come up for discussion.

SCHEDULE OF EXTENSION DEPARTMENT MEETINGS

FIRST WEEK: *Report Meeting*

Scripture reading and prayer (5 minutes)
Visitor's monthly written reports
Secretary's report on blackboard
(This will be a compilation of the reports from the visitors and should include at least six headings—the number of members, visits made, Sunday school lessons studied, daily Bible readers, amount of offering, and special kindnesses done for the members. The secretary analyzes the report.)
Oral reports of visitation experiences
Assignments of prospects and new members

SECOND WEEK: *Promotional Meeting—Planning and Training*

Scripture reading and prayer (5 minutes)
Plans for enlargement of membership
Checking on department and group Standards
Plans for training the workers
Study of how to visit effectively
Demonstrations on how to visit and how to enrol members
Plans and training for soul-winning
Discussing a book in the Church Study Course
(Encourage study by the individual plan)
Presenting special objects of church program
Planning Annual Extension Day in June
Plans for presentation of church budget in November
Making plans for Christmas gifts and visits

THIRD WEEK: *Lesson Preparation Meeting*

Scripture reading and prayer (5 minutes)
Distribution and preview of next month's *Home Life*

Study of the daily Bible readings and comments for the last week in the current issue of *Home Life*

Study of the Sunday school lesson for the last Sunday in the month

Discussion of needs which lessons can meet
(Since visits are made during the last week of the month, the discussion should center on how the lesson for the last Sunday will meet the needs of members. The daily Bible readings and comments should also be considered to see how they relate to specific needs.

Planning approaches for discussion of these passages with the members.

FOURTH WEEK: *General Information Meeting*

Scripture reading and prayer (5 minutes)

Reading and discussing excerpts from the Extension section of *The Sunday School Builder*.

Discussing the Extension article in *Home Life* and other articles related to Extension work

Gleaning suggestions from the program for the Extension conference, as outlined in the *Sunday School Bulletin*

Studying the Extension department leaflets

Using the book *The Extension Department Lifting Through Love* for reference

FIFTH WEEK: *Special Emphases Meeting*

Scripture reading and prayer (5 minutes)

Planning new Extension interest center and presenting promotional ideas

Planning a social meeting for workers

II. SEEK TEACHING IMPROVEMENT IN CLASS SCHOOLS

"But," someone may object, "the plans described above are for department Sunday schools and we have classes, not departments. Can we do anything during the teaching improvement period except have someone teach the lesson while the rest of us listen and take notes?" The answer is an emphatic yes!

1. *Department Procedures Must Be Adapted*

Every Sunday school, no matter how small, should have at least six functioning departments: Cradle Roll, Nursery, Beginner, Primary, Young People Away, and Extension. In fact, even a small school will probably need more than one Nursery department. At the weekly officers and teachers' meeting the workers in these departments should meet separately for the regular department session and teaching improvement period. The number of workers in each department will, of course, be limited, but the procedures already set forth can be effectively adapted by even two workers who meet as a department to plan for the next Sunday or the next week's work.

Combining departments is not effective as a regular procedure. There are infrequent occasions when a combination is profitable if it has been carefully planned for a specific purpose. At one time during the year, Cradle Roll and Nursery workers may meet together for a discussion of the Nursery procedures, so that workers from both departments may learn how to interpret these procedures when they visit in the homes. At another time workers with these two age groups could profitably meet for a study of the age-group objectives which both are working to reach. (These objectives are listed under "Nursery" in *The Curriculum Guide.*)

Nursery, Beginner, and Primary workers could profit from one or two joint meetings dealing with (1) the educational principles underlying activity teaching, and (2) how the activities planned for the various age groups take account of the increasing maturity of the child as he passes from one group to the next.

The Extension department and the Young People Away department will function in the class Sunday school just as they do in a larger school. The patterns for their work apply to a small corps of workers as well as to a large group.

As a general rule, the workers with Juniors, Intermediates, Young People, and Adults should meet separately by age groups. There will be at least two teachers for each age group plus substitute teachers. In each case, the two or more teachers for the age group can meet to examine the teaching suggestions in their literature and to decide how the suggestions will be adapted in their respective classes. Even though all use the Uniform lessons, the varying abilities, interests, and needs of members of the different age groups make the lesson for one group quite distinct from the lesson of another group.

There will be a few occasions when workers with Intermediates, Young People, and Adults may profitably meet together to discuss some educational principles which all need to grasp and apply more fully. Perhaps once or twice in a year these three groups may meet and study how the same Scripture passage is used to meet the distinctive needs of Intermediates, Young People, married Young People, young Adults, and older Adults. However, the regular practice should be for each age group to have its own meeting, even if only two workers are present.

2. *Limitations Heighten Obligation*

Those who teach in a nondepartment Sunday school do so under some disadvantages. But if they can teach on Sunday in a one-room building or in classrooms without department assembly space, they can come together on Wednesday and prepare to teach under the same circumstances. The very fact that they lack some of the facilities of the more fortunate teachers who have assembly space and separate rooms makes it even more important that they meet each Wednesday for a period of co-operative study and planning.

The problem which the workers in the class Sunday school have in regard to the suggestions given is somewhat like that of the housewife with a limited budget who shops at the supermarket. She must choose from the crowded shelves what she needs most and can use best within the limits of her purse. The very limitations demand greater care both in the purchase of the food and in its preparation for the table. The class Sunday school can have just as valuable and varied program for the teaching improvement period as the department school.

III. SHARE THE HOUR OF PRAYER

1. *The Prayer Meeting Must Be Preserved*

We sing "Sweet Hour of Prayer," yet, because of our absence from the prayer meeting, we may not taste of its sweetness. Who more than officers and teachers in the Sunday school need the refreshing and the empowering that come from the hour of prayer? Ministers are fond of saying that the prayer meeting should be the most significant single meeting of the church. Poor attendance on this meeting is consequently cause for alarm. The weekly officers and teachers' meeting can do much to vitalize the meeting and enlarge attendance.

2. *The Prayer Meeting Can Be Vitalized*

The presence of officers and teachers will contribute much to the prayer meeting; the prayer meeting will in turn contribute much to them. Having confronted their responsibilities and inadequacies, their problems for which they find no human solutions, their needs for which they in themselves have no supply, the Sunday school workers emerge from their several groups to join in the service of song and prayer and to find their source of power.

The prayer meeting may become the meeting for prayer, the "hour of power" which transforms officers and teachers into instruments "meet for the Master's use." Just as the Sunday school and the worship service on Sunday morning are the two halves of a whole, so the officers and teachers' meeting and the prayer meeting unite to form the midweek service which gives dynamic to every aspect of the life and ministry of the church.

IV. THE CHAPTER SUMMARIZED

1. Workers with Intermediates need to study together their special problems and responsibilities, to share their experiences and purposes, and to develop specific plans for increasingly fruitful teaching.

2. Workers with Young People should share their need of understanding of those whom they teach and plan cooperatively to make their teaching and guidance maximally effective.

3. Workers with Adults need one another's help in preparing and teaching lessons that will be informing, inspiring, enriching, and life-changing, following tested methods of lesson planning and presentation.

4. Extension workers have definite teaching opportunities and responsibilities and should confer each week as to procedures in making theirs a teaching ministry.

5. For the class Sunday school, the procedures described will require certain modifications, but they can readily be adapted to suit the conditions of the smaller school.

6. The prayer meeting, in some respects the most important meeting of the church, is an extension of the officers and teachers' meeting; each should re-enforce and vitalize the other.

CHAPTER 9

I. Increased Quality of Fruitage
   1. Quality Is Required
   2. Quality May Be Assured

II. Increased Quantity of Fruitage
   1. Growth Is Demanded
   2. The Means of Growth Are at Hand

III. Increased Laborers for the Harvest
   1. More Workers Are Needed
   2. Workers Must Be Discovered and Trained

IV. Increased Evangelistic Fruitage
   1. Education and Evangelism Are Inseparable
   2. Perennial Evangelism Can Be Maintained

V. Increased Enlistment Fruitage
   1. Nonenlistment Is a Tragic Fact
   2. Full Enlistment Should Be Achieved

IV. Increased Missionary Fruitage
   1. Missionary Indifference Can Be Cured
   2. Missionary Fruitage Can Be Borne

VII. Increased Stewardship Fruitage
   1. Stewardship Undergirds the Christian Enterprise
   2. Stewardship in a Church Must Be Developed

VIII. Increased Spiritual Fruitage
   1. Balance Between Spiritual and Material Must Be Maintained
   2. Temporal Means Must Be Used for Spiritual Ends

IX. The Chapter Summarized

9

The Weekly Officers and Teachers' Meeting Increases Fruitage

THE CALL of Christ is to increased fruitage. In the parable of the fig tree, Jesus taught that the fruitless tree might be given another chance, but if it still bore no fruit, it deserved to be cut down (Luke 13:6–9). He pronounced the doom of the fig tree which gave promise of fruit but bore "leaves only" (Matt. 21:19). He declared that "every tree that bringeth not forth good fruit is hewn down, and cast into the fire." Then he announced the basic principle: "Wherefore by their fruits ye shall know them" (Matt. 7:20).

Can we doubt that Jesus requires of his church, and of the Sunday school as its teaching agency, that it bear fruit that abides? The weekly officers and teachers' meeting has demonstrated its abiding worth through its ever-widening contribution to the increased fruitfulness of the Sunday school in many of the most important areas of church life and service. We conclude our study with an examination of these major opportunities of increased fruitfulness.

I. INCREASED QUALITY OF FRUITAGE

1. Quality Is Required

The Sunday school does not exist for its own sake. Like the tree to which Jesus refers, it is known by its fruits. The question which he raised must ever be ours: What kind of fruit? The fruit may be plentiful but of poor quality. That is, people may attend the Sunday school in large numbers, there may be signs of outward success, but lives may be little changed and the cause of Christ advanced scarcely at all.

Jesus speaks of salt that has lost its savour and is "thenceforth good for nothing" (Matt. 5:13). Is it possible for a Sunday school to be "good" yet "good for nothing"?

2. Quality May Be Assured

The coming together of officers and teachers week by week, under the direction of the general superintendent and department superintendents, with the pastor and minister of education present to guide, will of necessity raise the question of quality. Careless or incompetent officers and teachers will find their weaknesses brought to light and will be constrained either to improve or to resign. Pupils who take their Sunday school attendance and lessons lightly will find themselves challenged to serious consideration of the Sunday school as an educational enterprise and will almost certainly respond accordingly. The church will recognize the Sunday school as having responsibility to carry out its commission to teach and will provide for it adequately.

II. INCREASED QUANTITY OF FRUITAGE

1. Growth Is Demanded

Quantity is not the antithesis of quality. Jesus sought both qualitative and quantitative results as he taught the twelve. His devotion to the teaching of the few was to the end that through them he might reach the many. To the little congregation of believers, before his ascension, he gave the commission, "Ye shall be witnesses unto me both in Jerusalem, and in all Judaea, and in Samaria, and unto the uttermost part of the earth" (Acts 1:8). Pentecost gave ample proof of the intention of Jesus to win the many through the few.

2. The Means of Growth Are at Hand

The success of a Sunday school is not to be measured by the number enrolled but by the proportion of enrolment to possibilities. A Sunday school of one hundred, by this test, may be a greater Sunday school than one with an enrolment of a thousand. So long as there are unreached and untaught people of any age or condition anywhere, the business of the Sunday school is to try to reach and to teach them.

Such a standard calls for unceasing inquiry and concern. Ours is a moving population that makes the census of one year out of date the next. One of the most significant social facts of our generation is the increase of population.

Not a week should pass without a checkup on absentees and prospects, with plans for visitation and invitation. Officers and teachers who meet each week can plan effectually for enlargement and then put the plans into operation. Concerning these unreached multitudes it remains true, "They will not come, they must be sought; they will not learn, they must be taught." Concern for quality must be matched by equal concern for quantity.

III. Increased Laborers for the Harvest

Jesus, as he went about teaching, preaching, and healing, saw the unreached multitudes and had compassion on them. Then he said to his disciples, "The harvest truly is plenteous, but the labourers are few; pray ye therefore the Lord of the harvest, that he will send forth labourers into his harvest" (Matt. 9:37–38). As he still looks on the multitudes, scattered and shepherdless, is he not bidding us to pray for more laborers for the ripe and waiting harvest?

1. More Workers Are Needed

We know that the multitudes to be reached increase with each passing year. We know that Sunday school enrolment is not keeping pace with the increase of population. We know that for every worker added, we can, on the average, add ten more persons to Sunday school enrolment. We know that we can neither reach nor hold these new possibilities unless we have adequate, competent officers and teachers. The gravest need that we confront is the discovery and training of additional laborers for the harvest.

2. Workers Must Be Discovered and Trained

The weekly officers and teachers' meeting affords one of

the best opportunities for this discovery and training. The procedure is simple and practical:

(1) Let the church authorize the appointment of a personnel survey committee who will regularly and carefully study the entire church membership roll and will confer with the teachers of Young People and Adults, in order to discover those who have evident potential qualifications as Sunday school officers and teachers.

(2) Enrol these prospective workers in a training class which can meet at a time best suited to their convenience, preferably at the time of the weekly officers and teachers' meeting.

(3) This training class, meeting each week for at least three months, led by a capable person, will study an appropriate training course book (*Building a Standard Sunday School, A Church Using Its Sunday School, The Improvement of Teaching in the Sunday School,* or *Teaching to Win and Develop* or another basic book), with application of principles to the needs of the local situation.

(4) Members of the class will be familiarized with the work and materials of each of the several departments in order to discover the work for which they are best suited.

(5) Members of the class may on occasion serve as supply teachers and officers, thus getting actual practice.

(6) From this group the nominating committee can propose to the church for election persons who have had a measure of preparation for their important tasks.

This continuous program of initial training will give to the church an ever-enlarging "pool" of available and capable officers and teachers who are more necessary to "fruitage that remains" than any other human factor.

IV. INCREASED EVANGELISTIC FRUITAGE

1. *Education and Evangelism Are Inseparable*

Evangelism and education are twin heartbeats of a New Testament church. Whatever we do, we must keep in mind that it is "all for evangelism." To fail to evangelize is to fail.

If we are true to the New Testament pattern, we will precede evangelism with teaching and follow it with teaching. We are not saved by knowledge but salvation is not apart from knowledge. Jesus said, "And ye shall know the truth, and the truth shall make you free" (John 8:32).

Paul joined evangelism and Christian education inseparably in his convincing reasoning: "So then faith cometh by hearing, and hearing by the word of God" (Rom. 10:17).

Sunday school teachers should always have soul-winning as their objective. If there are unsaved persons in their classes, the teachers teach to win them to Christ. Since usually the majority are already saved, teachers teach to make their members bearers of a soul-winning witness. Since the unsaved multitudes are not in Sunday school, the business of officers and teachers is to lead their responsible members to go with Christ after the lost.

2. Perennial Evangelism Can Be Maintained

The fires of evangelism will burn low and even go out if they are not replenished with fuel. It is not enough—in a day when we must evangelize a generation best described as a procession—to rekindle the fire once a year at the time of the annual revival. Sin and death know no season; soul-winning should not be just occasional.

If this perennial business of the church is to be kept continuous, officers and teachers must let no week pass when they do not take account of their evangelistic responsibilities and opportunities. Churches with the greatest evangelistic fruitage bear glad testimony that they gain their best results through the soul-winning concern expressed and implemented in the weekly officers and teachers' meeting. No other plan equals it for the fruitage of souls.

V. INCREASED ENLISTMENT FRUITAGE

The only fruitage more gratifying than that of a saved soul is a saved soul plus a saved life. It is unfortunately true that many who have trusted Christ for salvation have not been enlisted in his service.

1. *Nonenlistment Is a Tragic Fact*

Averages are admittedly misleading; yet they can form a basis of comparison. Studies indicate that in a representative Southern Baptist church three out of ten members are non-resident; three out of ten are resident but inactive; two out of ten are partially enlisted; and two out of ten are fully faithful in the service and support of the church.

Taking a typical church of 300 members as example, this means that, on an average, 90 are nonresident; 90 are inactive, rarely if ever attending or giving or serving; 60 are partially enlisted, attending, serving, giving irregularly; 60 can be depended upon to attend the services regularly, serve in the work of the church faithfully, and give to the support of the church systematically and regularly. Think of what it would mean if the 50 per cent of partially enlisted and inactive members were as fully enlisted as the faithful 20 per cent, and the 30 per cent who are nonresident were reactivated through transfer of membership to churches where they now live!

Why do these many members thus become unfruitful? Perhaps some were never saved, but who are we to judge? The explanation may be that of the child who fell out of bed—he went to sleep too close to where he got in!

2. *Full Enlistment Should Be Achieved*

The question needs to be asked repeatedly, "After baptism —what?" The Sunday school offers the best reply: Become active in Bible study, take part in the affairs of class and department, prepare for effective church membership through the Training Union, and thus learn the joy and earn the reward of Christian service!

The solution of the enlistment problem is largely in the hands of Sunday school officers and teachers. Through their interest and efforts, every church member can be engaged not only in the study of the Bible but in some form of attractive and fruitful service. Why is this not more generally done? Not because of lack of interest and concern; rather, because there is no definite plan by which this opportunity and responsibility can be implemented.

When officers and teachers meet every week and plan together a program which calls for every-member participation, together with personal contacts to obtain this participation, they can effectively reduce the alarming incidence of unenlistment.

VI. INCREASED MISSIONARY FRUITAGE

1. *Missionary Indifference Can Be Cured*

"The mission of a church is missions!" Do we believe it? In the early history of Baptists of America, the majority were antimissionary. Three things accounted for this attitude—an overemphasis on the doctrine of election, the fear of "boards" and other forms of organization, and ignorance. Ignorance was then and is now the chief barrier to our worthy support of missions. "Not to be *up* on missions is to be *down* on missions," remains a true saying.

A Baptist becomes a missionary for two main reasons— understanding of the Bible and understanding of the desperate need of a lost world. Just as one cannot read the Bible with open mind and heart and not believe that our basic Baptist doctrines are true to its teaching, so one cannot read the Bible with simple acceptance of its authority and refuse to be missionary. Add to the clear command of Jesus a comprehension of the lost condition of more than one half the people of the world and the result is a missionary Baptist.

There are few if any outright antimissionary Baptists in our churches but there are many who are "omissionary." They are not concerned because they are not informed. The Sunday school is a major source of supply of needed missionary information and inspiration.

There are many lessons that are directly missionary in content. Every lesson should be taught with missionary spirit and in a missionary atmosphere.

The Standards, from the beginning, have carried a missionary emphasis. The current Standard reads:

1. The school shall present educationally each year the Co-operative Program.
2. The workers in the Sunday school shall encourage members to support the cause of Christ through the Cooperative Program.
3. At least three denominational causes, associational, state, and/or Convention-wide, shall be presented annually in the assembly periods.
4. The Sunday school offering shall be handled in accordance with the policy of the church.

As the church's inclusive teaching agency, the Sunday school will reinforce the missionary purposes and plans of the Training Union, the Woman's Missionary Union, and the Brotherhood. All of these organizations will work together to make the church vitally missionary in all its life and work. Every Sunday school worker should study the training course book, *The Sunday School and Missions.*

It is not enough for a church to give to "the Cooperative Program," as important as is this plan of giving for the proportionate support of all denominational causes. Each object must become a living thing. State, home, foreign missions must be seen as devoted missionaries winning the lost and extending the kingdom of God at home and abroad. Christian education must be seen as consecrated teachers preparing young people for Christian service. Hospitals and Children's Homes must be seen as ministering servants of Christ healing the sick and caring for unfortunate children. Editors and publishers and promoters of radio and television communication must be seen as men and women called of God to "publish glad tidings." The Annuity Board must be seen as warmhearted servants of Christ seeking to give protection and security to their needy fellow ministers.

2. *Missionary Fruitage Can Be Borne*

Through the weekly officers and teachers' meeting, missions and the Cooperative Program can thus be personalized. Plans can be made for missionary assembly programs and the observance of special missionary days. Prayer can be included at every meeting for specific causes represented in the

Cooperative Program. Missionary literature can be circulated; missionary pictures can be shown. Frequently the prayer meeting following the weekly officers and teachers' meeting may be devoted to missions. Annually there may be conducted a church school of missions, which Sunday school workers will support.

The fruitage of missions will appear in worthy and sacrificial giving, in the establishment and support of community missions, and best of all in the call of God to missionary service of the choicest of the church's young people. A church will assuredly be missionary if such emphasis as indicated is maintained week after week, year after year.

VII. Increased Stewardship Fruitage

1. *Stewardship Undergirds the Christian Enterprise*

Evangelism, enlistment, and missions are incomplete if not followed and supported by the teaching and the practice of Christian stewardship. The gospel is good news to the unsaved—salvation is offered freely on the simple terms of repentance toward God and faith in the Lord Jesus Christ. The gospel is also good news to the saved—life can be lived according to the will of God the owner and for the purposes of Jesus Christ the Saviour.

Evangelism is the proclamation of the gospel to the unsaved; stewardship is the practice of the gospel by the saved. Missions is the sending of the gospel to the lost; stewardship is the sending of the gospel to the lost by the saved. According to the New Testament, evangelism and missions are inseparable from stewardship. The saved are to share their salvation with others, far and near; this process of sharing is Christian stewardship.

The doctrine of Christian stewardship is that all of life belongs to God and is to be used according to his will for the purposes of Jesus Christ. This involves dedication of time, talents, influence, and possessions to service through the church. Such life dedication calls for the systematic giving of tithes and offerings.

The most signal failure of enlistment is in the area of stewardship. This failure is conspicuous in the matter of money. Church members who do not give systematically and proportionately through the church for its maintenance and for the support of its world-embracing mission are not likely to be vitally enlisted in other respects. Jesus said, "For where your treasure is, there will your heart be also" (Matt. 6:21).

2. *Stewardship in a Church Must Be Developed*

The Sunday school can largely determine the standard of stewardship of a church. Stewardship must be taught if it is to be practiced. It is effectively taught not only by words but through practice. Many churches have discovered that the Sunday school is the best agency by which to get the budget subscribed and through which to lead people to practice the New Testament principle, "Upon the first day of the week let every one of you lay by him in store, as God hath prospered him" (1 Cor. 16:2).

The use of the Sunday school as a means both for subscribing the budget and collecting the offerings is hardly possible without the weekly officers and teachers' meeting. At this meeting the doctrine of Christian stewardship can be clarified and emphasized. During the administrative and promotional periods, plans can be made for reaching every member and obtaining a worthy subscription. During the teaching improvement period, the doctrine of stewardship can be found implicit and explicit in many lessons and applied practically to the lives of members, from the youngest to the oldest. A church with a live officers and teachers' meeting, using its Sunday school for the teaching and the practice of stewardship, will effectually solve its financial problems.

VIII. INCREASED SPIRITUAL FRUITAGE

1. *Balance Between Spiritual and Material Must Be Maintained*

A church is a spiritual community, operating for spiritual purposes and by spiritual means. It is a "gathered community," its citizens being those who have been called out from sin to salvation, from darkness to light, from evil to righteousness, from death to life. It is spiritual in that its primary concern is for the soul, the imperishable part of man. The mark of its members is that "we look not at the things which are seen, but at the things which are not seen: for the things which are seen are temporal; but the things which are not seen are eternal" (2 Cor. 4:18). Just as the spirit of a man operates through his body, so a church functions through such material means as building, equipment, organization, money, and service—all for the sake of souls.

A church often finds it difficult to keep the material and the spiritual in proper balance. The words of Jesus are plain and well known: "Seek ye first the kingdom of God, and his righteousness; and all these things shall be added unto you" (Matt. 6:33). The admonition of Paul is also well understood: "Set your affection on things above, not on things on the earth" (Col. 3:2). Yet a church, like an individual, may find itself putting *things* first—building and budget, comfort and convenience, numbers and notice, prestige and power. There may be so much concern for efficient organization that the whir of the machinery drowns out the voice of the Spirit. How to make all things serve spiritual ends is every church's problem.

2. *Temporal Means Must Be Used for Spiritual Ends*

The Sunday school is effective in keeping the spiritual and the material in proper proportion. A new or enlarged or improved building may be needed, but only as it serves the spiritual purposes of worship, teaching, training, winning, serving. More adequate equipment may be needed, but only as it makes possible more fruitful ministries. More money from more people may be needed, but only as its giving develops the givers and its use increases the love for God and for the needy at home and around the world. Preaching is, of course, indispensable in maintaining this perspective, but preaching without the support of effective teaching will rarely achieve its purpose.

The weekly officers and teachers' meeting, supporting and supported by the prayer meeting, can do much to keep spiritual values uppermost. The fellowship of the meeting will deepen the spiritual lives of pastor and officers and teachers as they think and plan and study and pray together. Absorbed in temporal pursuits as many are, they are very likely to bring worldly-mindedness rather than spiritual-mindedness to their church work. In the companionship of those who have more of the mind of the Spirit, officers and teachers who are less inclined to the spiritual will be more likely to change their attitudes and put the emphasis where the Bible clearly would have it. "And let us consider one another to provoke unto love and to good works" (Heb. 10:24).

Nowhere may the pastor's spiritual influence be more effectually exerted than in these weekly meetings of Sunday school officers and teachers, as he leads them to put first things first, to entrust themselves to the Holy Spirit's guidance, and to make the objective of all their preparation, organization, teaching, and personal work the growing of a Spirit-filled church whose members are bearing the fruit of the Spirit—"love, joy, peace, longsuffering, gentleness, goodness, faith, meekness, temperance" (Gal. 5:22-23).

This study could scarcely close better than with this appeal to maintain the church of Jesus Christ, "which he hath purchased with his own blood," as a spiritual body. Alongside the pastor, the minister of education, and the general superintendent, Sunday school officers and teachers are responsible for the purity and welfare of the church. As the pastor ministers and preaches and as his fellow workers in the Sunday school lead and teach, so will the church grow spiritually and fulfil its spiritual mission. Coming together week by week, with this high purpose always in view, the pastor and his colaborers can progressively build a church, with Christ Jesus himself as the chief cornerstone, "in whom the whole structure is joined together and grows into a holy temple in the Lord; in whom you also are built into it for a dwelling place of God in the Spirit" (Eph. 2:21-22 RSV).

IX. THE CHAPTER SUMMARIZED

1. Christ's requirement of qualitative results calls for our best efforts to make the Sunday school a *school* worthy of its name.

2. Christ's quantitative standard includes the requirement of growth, which should be continuous until every possible person has been reached.

3. The key to higher quality and increased numbers is the personnel of responsible workers, who must be discovered and trained for their work.

4. The New Testament makes education and evangelism inseparable and through this vital relationship perennial evangelism will be maintained.

5. The solution of the otherwise baffling problem of non-enlistment of church members is largely in the hands of Sunday school officers and teachers, through whom can be achieved the ideal of a place for every member and every member in his place.

6. The blight of missionary indifference finds its effectual cure through the teaching of missions that results in conviction and practical expression.

7. Evangelism, enlistment, and missions are undergirded by Christian stewardship, which must be so taught that it will be believed and practiced.

8. The supreme objectives of a church are spiritual, for which all its temporal means exist, made effectual through human instrumentalities divinely endued and led.

SUGGESTIONS FOR THE TEACHER

WHO WILL LEAD IN THE STUDY OF THIS BOOK

TEACHING AIM: *To lead class members to discover how to make more effective use of the weekly officers and teachers' meeting as a means of implementing the spiritual ministry of the Sunday school.*

INFORMATION TO BE SECURED: What type of school, or schools, will be represented in the class? Which hold weekly officers and teachers' meetings? What is the attitude of the leaders in each school toward the weekly officers and teachers' meeting? What do they consider are the main difficulties in maintaining such a meeting? How should the study of this book be guided to help overcome these difficulties?

MOTIVATION: Some class members may come with a smug attitude, some with disheartened spirits, and some with enthusiasm and eagerness to improve their situation. Seek to help all to see the spiritual implications of the present study. Suggest that the business of a church, and therefore of a Sunday school, is to lead people to become Christians and then to help each one to be Christian. Comment that the functions of a Sunday school, while centering in Bible teaching, are becoming quite comprehensive. Propose the claim that a functioning weekly officers and teachers' meeting will help a Sunday school to achieve everything that it needs to achieve in order to fulfil its mission.

SCHEDULING: If your class consists of people who have had some experience with a weekly officers and teachers' meeting you will wish to reduce the time given to the early chapters. If chapters 1–5 can be covered in two nights, or four forty-five-minute periods, extra time can be given to the study of plan sheets and to the demonstration and its evaluation, as suggested for chapters 6, 7, 8.

Chapter 1

Before the class period, list on a chalkboard, poster, or flip-chart, the eight statements in the first eight headings of the chapter outline. Have them covered. Uncover the first statement. Let the class read it. Ask if they believe it. Lead them to analyze its significance and its bearing on their own church program.

Uncover II and have it read. Give a summary of Dr. Dobbins' discussion.

Uncover III, have it read, and ask members to prove, or disprove, the statement. Have the class read Matthew 4:23; 9:35; 28:19-20. Add other references of your own selection.

Uncover IV. After it is read, explain the danger of "fragmentation." Have class members read the sentences in the first five lines of page 6. Compare with the statement of the business of a church which appears in the foregoing paragraph on motivation.

Uncover V. Ask: Do you believe it? Justify your answer. After responses, add any major ideas from pages 6–7 which seem to have been overlooked.

Use VI, VII, VIII in a similar manner. Have the class turn to page 11 and read the chapter summary.

PROPOSE: If we agree that building a better Sunday school results in building a better church, what should be our objective in this study? Lead members to formulate an objective which is acceptable to the class.

Chapter 2

Secure the latest filmstrip on the weekly officers and teachers' meeting. Before showing it, ask members to look for all the values of the weekly officers and teachers' meeting mentioned or implied in the filmstrip. After the showing compile a list of points the class mentions. (Most of these will be discussed in later chapters, so they may just be listed at this time.) Comment briefly that this list shows that the advantages of a weekly officers and teachers' meeting far outweigh the difficulties in the way of maintaining such a meeting.

If the list made by the class contains the words fellowship, planning, and sharing, encircle these words. If not, write them. Encourage class members to point out how the weekly officers and teachers' meeting supplies each of these needs. Supplement their comments by your own presentation of the points made by the author under III, IV, V, in the chapter outline.

ASK: What are the difficulties in the way of holding a weekly officers and teachers' meeting in your church? Encourage free, frank replies. Then lead the group to face each difficulty mentioned as you point out briefly that it can be overcome.

Mention the workshop procedure planned for chapters 3 and 4. State the main problem to be dealt with in each, and ask members to give some forethought to the matter.

Chapter 3

Use a workshop procedure in which the class is led to consider the seven statements which constitute outline headings I through VII as a self-measurement test. Regarding each ask: To what extent do the weekly officers and teachers' meetings in your church measure up to this aspect of good planning? If responses seem slow, use questions to draw out from prepared members the meaning of the point in question. Then compare the author's comments with what the church is doing. Considering any weaknesses brought out in this analysis, major on a discussion of how the church can improve.

If this book is being studied in a church which is not holding a weekly officers and teachers' meeting, let this chapter guide the group as they plan how to start one and make it succeed.

Chapter 4

Note the chapter purpose stated on page 45. Challenge the class to note every suggestion they find which would add to the effectiveness of the promotional part of the weekly officers and teachers' meeting in their church. Display the chapter outline. After a discussion of the contents of the chapter, class members should compile recommendations for the improvement of the administration and promotional ministry of the weekly officers and teachers' meetings in their own church or their respective churches. These recommendations should be specific in respect to the use made of records, the schedule followed in the meeting, and the use of the plans made during Preparation Week.

Assign the reports suggested for chapter 5.

Chapter 5

Note that the first eight main points in the chapter outline deal with eight requisites for better teaching, while point IX in the chapter outline deals with other means of improvement. Point out how the teaching improvement period of the weekly officers and teachers' meeting can be used to secure or develop each of these requisites. You may wish to assign these nine points to nine members who will use two or three minutes each to report on what the author has brought out. They should comment on the value of his suggestions as a means of improving teaching in their respective situations. Use the rest of the time for a round-table discussion of how the suggestions in this chapter may be

written into weekly officers and teachers' meeting plans and training plans for the year so that the eight requisites for better teaching may be cared for in logical order and with balanced emphasis.

If the filmstrips in the "Teacher Improvement Series" are
available, a committee of department superintendents may be
asked to view these and report on how the filmstrips will fit into
the tentative schedule of training emphasis for the year which
the class has prepared.

Chapter 6

Display chapter outline. Have the group read the seven main
heads for statements of seven possible procedures for a teaching
improvement period. Ask: Which of these procedures have you
used or seen used? Considering the procedures one by one, ask
for testimonies as to how each has been used, the values which
resulted, and the weaknesses noted. If the methods reported or
the evaluations given vary greatly from the suggestions by Dr.
Dobbins, call attention to the variation and let the class discuss
the relative merits of Dr. Dobbins' suggested procedure and the
one which has been reported.

In preparation for the next class period, distribute plan sheets.
Ask the members to study them and to be ready to point out how
they would be used in a teaching improvement period. Sample
plan sheets are given in a number of the superintendents' man-
uals and the books on teaching which relate to specific age groups.
Sample copies can usually be obtained on request to the proper
age group superintendent in the Sunday School Department of
the Baptist Sunday School Board. Or, plan sheets can be prepared by spacing out the points listed on page 87, allowing room
under each for suggestions to be written in. Variations in these
plan sheets are needed for Cradle Roll and Extension workers.
See the literature for these age groups for forms that may be
followed.

Chapters 7 and 8

You may wish to use a partial demonstration of a weekly officers
and teachers' meeting in which all class members participate.

1. Make brief comments about the values of a fellowship meal.

2. Have the class follow the schedule on page 93 as you review
briefly what will be done in the general promotional period—
noting especially the discussion under headings III and IV.

3. Note the eight things to be cared for in the promotional

period in the department and ask how the list would be modified to suit each of the various age groups, including the Cradle Roll and Extension departments.

4. Illustrate the use of plan sheets, have copies reproduced for each age group. Let class members meet in small groups according to the ages taught in Sunday school. Have them use the plan sheets in an effort to plan next week's lesson. There may not be time to complete the plans, but the workers should be able to get the idea of how plan sheets are used. (If plan sheets are not available, each planning group may follow the appropriate pattern as suggested on pp. 100–105 or p. 108.)

Have a department superintendent designated in advance to preside in each group. To supplement the suggestions in these chapters, supply each of these leaders with the literature giving suggestions for the teaching improvement in the department he represents.

5. In the second class period lead each group to report on the experiences they had in their "teaching improvement sessions" and to comment on the usefulness of their plan sheets.

If this book is being studied in a class Sunday school, adapt the foregoing suggestions to demonstrate a teaching improvement period in which workers meet by age groups and plan for next Sunday, using the plan sheets (with adaptations as needed).

Chapter 9

Comment on the author's use of the term "fruitage." Ask class members to mention ways in which the weekly officers and teachers' meeting leads to "increased fruitage." List the responses made by class members.

As the class follows the chapter outline, briefly but forcefully present the fruitage which may be expected as the result of an effective weekly officers and teachers' meeting.

ASK: What are you willing to do to insure such fruitage? Let this question lead members to volunteer statements about specific things they will do, individually and as a group, to make the weekly officers and teachers' meeting an effective tool for building a better Sunday school.

Some Suggested Visual Materials

In addition to the filmstrips already suggested, you may wish to use the filmstrips on the work of the various age groups, selecting from each the frames which show the weekly officers and teachers' meeting.

For supplementary material you may show the filmstrips: *Laws of Sunday School Growth, Using Filmstrips in the Church,* and *Using Records Effectively.*

FOR REVIEW AND WRITTEN WORK

CHAPTER 1

1. Why is teaching necessary to the growth and development of Christian character?
2. How could your Sunday school promote greater unity in the program of your church?
3. To what extent is your church fully enlisting its members? How could the Sunday school increase enlistment?

CHAPTER 2

4. List the values of the weekly officers and teachers' meeting as set forth in this chapter. Check the three which seem to you most important for your situation.
5. What objections are frequently raised to the weekly officers and teachers' meetings? How may they be overcome?

CHAPTER 3

6. Why should the weekly officers and teachers' meeting be established and controlled by the church?
7. Why are convinced officers and teachers prerequisite to the success of the weekly officers and teachers' meeting?
8. Who should be expected to attend the weekly officers and teachers' meeting? How may each person be led to accept the obligation as a privilege?

CHAPTER 4

9. How does the weekly officers and teachers' meeting provide a means of effective co-operation?
10. What matters of promotion should be cared for each week through the weekly officers and teachers' meeting?
11. What would be the most suitable schedule for the officers and teachers' meeting in your church?

CHAPTER 5

12. How can personal improvement be secured through the weekly officers and teachers' meeting?
13. How can the weekly officers and teachers' meeting help teachers to secure a working knowledge of the Bible?

14. How may pupil study be encouraged and guided through the weekly officers and teachers' meeting?

15. How may a thorough grasp of the principles of teaching be developed through the meeting?

CHAPTER 6

16. What preparation must the department superintendent make for conducting a successful teaching improvement period? State two tests of such a period.

17. Name seven ways in which the teaching improvement period may be conducted. Why is variety necessary?

18. State what you consider the strongest point in favor of each of these plans for conducting the teaching improvement period: (1) previous assignment method, (2) the demonstration lesson method, (3) the teaching principles method, (4) the plan sheet method.

CHAPTER 7

19. In what practical ways can attendance and growth be promoted through the weekly officers and teachers' meeting? How can planned visitation be secured?

20. Why should the most important aspect of the weekly meeting be the teaching improvement period?

CHAPTER 8

21. How may the teaching improvement period in a class Sunday school be profitably conducted?

22. Show how the weekly officers and teachers' meeting may strengthen and improve the prayer meeting.

23. Select one of the departments, or age groups, and list the items (from this or the preceding chapter) which should be included in the plan sheet or suggested guidance outline for planning the teaching procedure for that age group.

CHAPTER 9

24. How will a functioning weekly officers and teachers' meeting help to assure increase in both the quantity and the quality of the results attained in a Sunday school?

25. How does the teaching ministry of a church relate to its missionary and stewardship spirit?